LUXURY UNVEILED

Luxury Unveiled

Inside Five-Star Excellence

MACK RAFEAL

Kellie D. Sikora

Contents

INDEX	1
Chapter 1	3
Chapter 2	19
Chapter 3	37
Chapter 4	57
Chapter 5	74
Chapter 6	92
Chapter 7	112
Chapter 8	129
Chapter 9	148

INDEX

Chapter 1: Introduction
1.1 Setting the Stage
1.2 Definition of Luxury
1.3 Evolution of Luxury in History
1.4 Significance of Five-Star Excellence

Chapter 2: The Art of Hospitality
2.1 The Foundation of Five-Star Service
2.2 Crafting Memorable Experiences
2.3 Importance of Personalization
2.4 Training the Exceptional Staff

Chapter 3: Architectural Splendor
3.1 Designing Elegance
3.2 Iconic Structures and Interiors
3.3 Fusion of Tradition and Modernity
3.4 Sustainability in Luxury Architecture

Chapter 4: Culinary Mastery
4.1 Gastronomic Delights
4.2 Michelin-Starred Dining
4.3 Celebrity Chefs and Signature Menus
4.4 Culinary Innovation in Luxury Hospitality

Chapter 5: Unveiling Exclusive Amenities
5.1 Beyond the Ordinary
5.2 Private Spas and Wellness Retreats
5.3 Personalized Concierge Services

5.4 Cutting-Edge Technological Features

Chapter 6: The World of High-End Accommodations
6.1 Luxurious Suites and Villas
6.2 Opulent Bedrooms and Lavish Bathrooms
6.3 Tailored In-Room Experiences
6.4 Privacy and Security in Five-Star Residences

Chapter 7: Exquisite Entertainment and Events
7.1 Grand Celebrations
7.2 Hosting Elite Gatherings
7.3 Exclusive Events and Entertainment
7.4 Redefining Extravagance in Social Functions

Chapter 8: The Business of Luxury
8.1 The Economics Behind Five-Star Excellence
8.2 Marketing Strategies for High-End Hospitality
8.3 Navigating Challenges in Luxury Management
8.4 Trends and Forecasts in Luxury Travel

Chapter 9: Beyond the Facade
9.1 Ethical Luxury
9.2 Social Responsibility in High-End Hospitality
9.3 Environmental Sustainability
9.4 Balancing Opulence with Purpose

Chapter 1

Introduction

Extravagance, a slippery domain of plushness and refinement, has long enraptured the human soul. It appears in different structures, from perfect craftsmanship and selective encounters to extravagant environmental factors that animate the faculties. In the fantastic embroidery of lavish living, the five-star space remains as a zenith of refinement and extravagance. This domain rises above the customary, winding around together a story of esteem, solace, and unrivaled help. As we leave on an excursion into this rarified air, we dig into the actual pith of what makes these safe-havens of quality so charming and respected.

The charm of a five-star experience lies not just in that frame of mind of its facilities, but rather in the fastidious scrupulousness that pervades each feature of its presence. From the second one stages across the edge, a cautiously organized vibe envelopes the guest, submerging them in this present reality where style isn't simply a quality however a lifestyle. The environmental factors, be they bombastic halls enhanced with rich crystal fixtures or personal suites decorated with custom goods, are intended to bring out a feeling of stunningness and miracle. It is a world carefully designed to take special care of the most insightful preferences, where every component is a demonstration of the commitment flawlessly.

Key to the appeal of five-star extravagance is the obligation to unrivaled assistance. Past the unmistakable features of riches, it is the immaterial motions — the expectant help, the customized consideration — that hoist the experience to unprecedented levels. It is the consistent organization of a complicated expressive dance of administration experts, each receptive to the novel requirements of the visitor, that changes a simple stay into a critical stay. This obligation to support greatness is the foundation whereupon the standing of these foundations is constructed, cultivating an environment where each impulse isn't just expected yet surpassed.

The culinary scene inside the limits of five-star extravagance is a gastronomic ensemble, where unbelievable cooks coordinate culinary enjoyments that rise above simple food. From Michelin-featured cafés to hint bistros, the eating experience turns into a tactile excursion, where flavors dance on the sense of taste and show is a fine art. The culinary groups inside these sanctuaries of gastronomy are craftsmans, winding around a story with each dish, using the best fixings to make an extraordinary luxurious encounter. It is a demonstration of the obligation to greatness that saturates each part of the five-star insight.

However, the charm of five-star extravagance reaches out past the limits of sumptuous facilities and luscious food. A vivid encounter stretches out to health and unwinding, welcoming visitors to loosen up in a desert spring of serenity. Spa withdraws inside these foundations are asylums where master advisors spoil the body and alleviate the brain, using respected procedures and state of the art medicines. It is an all encompassing way to deal with prosperity, recognizing the interconnectedness of body, brain, and soul, and offering a break from the chaotic speed of current life.

In the domain of five-star extravagance, each component, regardless of how apparently irrelevant, is a brushstroke on the material of guilty pleasure. The plan of a room, the determination of cloths, the fragrance that pervades the air — all add to the tactile orchestra that characterizes the visitor experience. It is a tender loving care that is firm, where even the most moment perspectives are thought of and refined flawlessly. The outcome is a climate that rises above the ordinary, shipping visitors to an existence where extravagance isn't simply a name yet a condition.

The charm of five-star extravagance isn't restricted to a specific geological area or social milieu. It is a worldwide peculiarity, rising above borders and consistently mixing social impacts to make an all inclusive language of richness. Whether settled in the core of a clamoring city or roosted on the quiet shores of a disconnected island, these shelters of extravagance share a consistent idea — an unfaltering obligation to giving an unrivaled encounter to the insightful explorer.

As we investigate the subtleties of five-star extravagance, it becomes obvious that it's anything but a static idea however a dynamic and developing articulation of refinement. The meaning of extravagance is molded by moving social standards, arising patterns, and the steadily developing assumptions for a complex customers. What was once viewed as the encapsulation of richness may now be viewed as a simple forerunner higher than ever of excess. In this consistently evolving scene, the quest for extravagance turns into an excursion of disclosure, an investigation of the limits of guilty pleasure.

The effect of innovation on the five-star experience can't be put into words. In a time where availability is foremost, these foundations flawlessly coordinate state of the art innovation into the visitor experience, from savvy room controls to vivid virtual attendant services. The combination of innovation and extravagance stretches out past simple comfort; it turns into an agreeable marriage that upgrades the general insight, permitting visitors to explore their environmental factors easily while keeping an air of restrictiveness.

The idea of supportability has likewise tracked down its direction into the core of five-star extravagance. As natural awareness develops, so too does the assumption that extravagance can coincide amicably with mindful stewardship of the planet.

From eco-accommodating practices in development and tasks to obtaining nearby, natural elements for culinary contributions, these foundations are progressively aware of their biological impression. The marriage of extravagance and maintainability not just fulfills the needs of a socially cognizant customers yet additionally starts a trend for the fate of rich living.

The charm of five-star extravagance reaches out past the singular explorer to include corporate substances looking for scenes that mirror their obligation to greatness. The matter of extravagance friendliness isn't restricted to giving an agreeable bed and wonderful cooking; it stretches out to establishing a climate helpful for undeniable level talks, vital preparation, and consistent execution of corporate occasions. The meeting offices inside these foundations are outfitted with cutting edge innovation and proposition a degree of administration that befits the height of those familiar with the better things throughout everyday life.

As we dive further into the universe of five-star extravagance, it becomes obvious that the excursion is basically as significant as the objective. The idea of experiential extravagance has acquired unmistakable quality, with explorers looking for something beyond material richness. The craving for one of a kind, vivid encounters has led to organized schedules that go past the bounds of the lodging walls, permitting visitors to investigate the rich embroidery of nearby culture, history, and regular marvels. The limits between the extravagance foundation and the objective haze, making a consistent coordination that improves the general insight.

The universe of five-star extravagance isn't safe to the unavoidable trends that range across the worldwide scene. The difficulties presented by monetary variances, international movements, and unexpected worldwide occasions require versatility and flexibility. However, it is unequivocally despite misfortune that the genuine determination of these foundations is tried. The capacity to weather conditions storms, turn despite vulnerability, and arise more grounded addresses the getting through tradition of five-star extravagance as a stronghold of soundness and faithful obligation to greatness.

In the terrific embroidery of extravagant living, five-star foundations stand as signals of lavishness, offering a safe-haven for the people who look for a departure from the conventional. As we explore the maze of guilty pleasure, from the lavish facilities to the gastronomic enjoyments, from the comprehensive health contributions to the consistent mix of innovation, we reveal an existence where each component is created flawlessly. The charm of five-star extravagance lies in the unmistakable articulations of lavishness as well as in the elusive snapshots of unmatched help, where each visitor isn't simply a supporter however a valued member in an orchestra of guilty pleasure.

In the sections that follow, we set out on a definite investigation of the different features that comprise the substance of five-star extravagance. From the building wonders that house these sanctuaries of lavishness to the culinary encounters that entice the taste buds, from the customized administration that surpasses assumptions to the developing scene of

maintainability, every part strips back the layers to uncover the complicated operations of an existence where extravagance isn't simply a superficial point of interest yet a way of thinking of life. Go along with us on this excursion into the core of extravagance, where everything about a disclosure, and each second is a festival of the remarkable.

1.1 Setting the Stage

In the amazing embroidered artwork of extravagance, the setting is the stage whereupon the show of lavishness unfurls. The actual indication of a five-star insight, the setting incorporates design wonders that stand as demonstrations of human resourcefulness and inventive vision. Whether settled in the core of a clamoring city, roosted on the quiet shores of an outlandish island, or tucked away in the serenity of a lavish open country, every five-star foundation is an exceptional articulation of its environmental elements and the social milieu wherein it lives.

Design brightness is a sign of five-star extravagance, rising above simple usefulness to turn into a visual orchestra that enthralls the faculties. From famous high rises that penetrate the metropolitan horizon to suggest shop inns that mix flawlessly with their regular environmental factors, the structural variety inside the domain of extravagance friendliness is immense. Engineers and creators team up to make spaces that fill a useful need as well as bring out feelings, recounting to a story that unfurls with each passing passage and each organized space.

The glory of the anteroom is in many cases the underlying experience with the universe of extravagance. Here, structural wonderfulness merges with inside plan to make a space that invites visitors with a feeling of stunningness. High roofs, rich ceiling fixtures, and carefully created goods set the vibe for the whole experience. The hall isn't just a temporary space; an introduction to the guilty pleasure anticipates inside. A space welcomes visitors to stop, calmly inhale, and drench themselves in the mood of extravagance.

The visitor rooms inside a five-star foundation are safe-havens of solace and refinement. The plan reasoning reaches out past style to incorporate usefulness and the consistent mix of innovation. These confidential retreats are fastidiously selected, with custom decorations, rich materials, and conveniences that take special care of the most insightful preferences. Whether offering all encompassing perspectives on city horizons or segregated vistas of regular ponders, the visitor rooms are intended to casing visitors in an environment of serenity and guilty pleasure.

The different design styles utilized in extravagance cordiality mirror a cognizant work to make a remarkable personality for every foundation. From the traditional polish of neoclassical plans to the smooth innovation of contemporary designs, the compositional language is an impression of the qualities and desires of the property. The outside veneers are materials whereupon the character of the foundation is painted, making way for the vivid experience that exists in.

The reconciliation of nature into the building configuration is a repetitive topic in extravagance cordiality. Whether it's the utilization of supportable materials, the consolidation of green spaces, or the consistent mixing of indoor and open air spaces, the normal world is in many cases a vital piece of the setting. Foundations arranged in beautiful areas influence their environmental factors, making a vivid encounter where the limit between the man-made and the normal is obscured.

The cooperative energy among engineering and inside plan is an essential part of the setting, molding the general tasteful and feeling of the foundation. Inside spaces are organized with an insightful eye, with fashioners choosing goods, variety ranges, and style that orchestrate with the engineering vision. The outcome is a climate where each component, from the selection of textures to the arrangement of craftsmanship, adds to the firm account of extravagance.

Past the visual charm, the setting additionally incorporates the environment and mood that penetrate the air. Lighting assumes a vital part in making the right state of mind, whether it's the warm sparkle of unpretentious enlightenment in private feasting spaces or the sensational play of light in extensive public regions. The exchange of light and shadow is a painstakingly arranged dance that upgrades the tangible experience, welcoming visitors to submerge themselves completely in the climate of extravagance.

The setting stretches out past the bounds of the actual space to remember the social and authentic setting for which the foundation is arranged. Lavish lodgings frequently draw motivation from the rich embroidered artwork of neighborhood legacy, injecting components of culture and history into their plan. Whether it's the fuse of conventional themes, the utilization of native materials, or organizations with neighborhood specialists, these foundations endeavor to make a feeling of spot that resounds with visitors.

The idea of extravagance isn't static; it develops in light of moving social standards and arising patterns. The setting turns into a material for the investigation of groundbreaking thoughts and articulations of extravagance. As the world hugs a more comprehensive way to deal with prosperity, the setting integrates health into its plan, with spa offices, wellness focuses, and wellbeing withdraws consistently coordinated into the general insight. The setting turns into a safe-haven for the brain, body, and soul, offering visitors an all encompassing departure from the afflictions of current life.

In the period of innovation, the setting isn't immaculate by the computerized upset. Shrewd room controls, intuitive showcases, and virtual attendant services are consistently coordinated into the texture of extravagance neighborliness. The utilization of innovation reaches out past simple comfort; it turns into an instrument to improve the general visitor experience, considering more noteworthy personalization and customization. The setting, in this computerized age, is a unique space that adjusts to the consistently changing necessities and inclinations of the insightful explorer.

As the world wrestles with the difficulties of maintainability, the setting of extravagance foundations mirrors a rising obligation to mindful stewardship of the climate. Green structure rehearses, energy-productive advances, and eco-accommodating drives are becoming vital parts of the setting. The rich scenes encompassing these foundations are not simply elaborate; they are painstakingly supported biological systems that add to the general supportability ethos.

The setting of extravagance friendliness is a no nonsense element that develops with the times. It is an impression of the qualities and desires of both the foundation and the visitors it takes special care of. As we explore the passages, relax in the halls, and look out from the galleries of five-star foundations, we are not simply seeing design splendor; we are venturing into a cautiously organized existence where everything about, subtlety, adds to the ensemble of extravagance. The setting isn't a scenery yet a functioning member in the vivid experience, making way for an excursion into extravagance.

1.2 Definition of Luxury

The meaning of extravagance is a nuanced and developing idea that rises above simple realism. It is a diverse articulation of extravagance, incorporating a rich embroidery of encounters, items, and ways of life that go past the normal. At its center, extravagance is an exemplification of eliteness, outstanding quality, and the quest for joy. As we dig into the multifaceted layers of this term, it becomes obvious that extravagance is definitely not a static element however a dynamic and emotional articulation that shifts across societies, people, and ages.

By and large, extravagance has been related with overflow, extraordinariness, and the ownership of significant merchandise. In antiquated developments, the first class displayed their status through belongings like valuable metals, gemstones, and complicatedly made relics. The shortage of these things and the craftsmanship put resources into their creation stamped them as images of wealth and differentiation. This verifiable point of view establishes the groundwork for the cutting edge comprehension of extravagance as something intriguing, selective, and frequently out of reach for the general population.

In the contemporary setting, the meaning of extravagance has extended to envelop a wide exhibit of components past unmistakable belongings. Encounters, for example, have turned into a significant feature of extravagance, with people looking for material richness as well as snapshots of guilty pleasure and recreation. The capacity to participate in remarkable and vital encounters, whether it be a personal ship outing, a connoisseur eating occasion, or a social submersion, is progressively seen as an extravagance in itself.

The idea of time as an extravagance highlights this change in context. In a quick moving existence where time is in many cases considered a valuable item, the advantage of recreation and the opportunity to seek after one's interests at a casual speed have become exceptionally esteemed. This transient component of extravagance is clear in the prevalence of selective get-aways, health withdraws, and the interest for customized, slow encounters.

The thought of extravagance is unpredictably attached to craftsmanship and the authority of abilities. High quality items, whether it be high fashion pieces of clothing, distinctive gems, or custom tailored furnishings, are worshipped for the careful meticulousness and the mastery put resources into their creation. The work serious nature of craftsmanship, combined with the uncommonness of hand tailored merchandise, adds to their restrictiveness and positions them at the apex of extravagance.

In the domain of design, extravagance isn't only about clothing yet a proclamation of singularity and wisdom. Top of the line style houses, with their famous logos and legacy, represent a pledge to quality, development, and a specific way of life. The charm of extravagance style lies in the articles of clothing themselves as well as in the stories they weave, the imaginativeness they address, and the societal position they present.

The auto business gives one more focal point through which to investigate the meaning of extravagance. Past the utilitarian capability of transportation, extravagance vehicles are permeated with state of the art innovation, choice plan, and a degree of solace that changes the demonstration of crashing into a liberal encounter. The responsibility for extravagance vehicle stretches out past reasonableness to imply a specific way of life and an assertion of progress.

In the domain of land, extravagance homes are described by their size and richness as well as by their area, engineering plan, and the selectiveness of their conveniences. The idea of a lavish home stretches out past sheer area to incorporate highlights, for example, all encompassing perspectives, best in class home computerization, and confidential admittance to sporting offices. The home turns into an impression of individual taste and a safe-haven of solace and refinement.

The cordiality business, especially five-star inns and resorts, is a stronghold of extravagance encounters. These foundations curate a climate where each component, from the building plan to the customized administration, adds to a feeling of lavishness. The advantage of convenience goes past simple solace to incorporate vivid encounters, gastronomic enjoyments, and health contributions that take special care of the comprehensive prosperity of visitors.

The meaning of extravagance is additionally formed by the immaterial parts of life, like protection and restrictiveness. Confidential individuals' clubs, select occasions, and celebrity admittance to desired encounters are sought-after extravagances that furnish people with a feeling of honor and differentiation. The selectiveness of such open doors supports that extravagance isn't just about what one has yet additionally about what one can get to.

The development of the computerized age has achieved a change in perspective in the manner extravagance is seen and consumed. The virtual domain offers new roads for encountering and exhibiting richness. From virtual style shows to computerized craftsmanship assortments, extravagance has expanded its venture into the computerized space, making a harmonious connection between the unmistakable and the virtual. Online entertainment stages become arranged features for people to show their sumptuous ways of life, further obscuring the lines between the physical and the computerized.

While the outward indications of extravagance differ, an ongoing idea that goes through its assorted articulations is the close to home effect it grants. Extravagance isn't only about having costly things; it is about the feelings, goals, and status that these belongings bring out. The brain research of extravagance utilization is complicated, driven by a longing for self-articulation, social acknowledgment, and the quest for an upgraded personal satisfaction.

As social orders advance, so too does the meaning of extravagance. The qualities and goals of a culture impact what is thought of as extravagant at some random time. In contemporary society, there is a developing accentuation on manageability and moral practices. The meaning of extravagance is growing to incorporate items and encounters that line up with ecologically cognizant qualities. Eco-accommodating materials, mindful obtaining, and a promise to social obligation are progressively viewed as markers of genuine extravagance.

The democratization of extravagance is another imperative pattern molding its definition. With the ascent of available extravagance marks, a more extensive section of the populace can participate in the experience of plushness. Extravagance is not generally restricted to a tip top scarcely any; it is presently open to a more different purchaser base. This democratization is reflected in the fame of reasonable extravagance things, from creator joint efforts to premium items with a more feasible price tag.

The elements of extravagance are additionally affected by social variety. What is viewed as an extravagance in one culture might vary fundamentally from another. The worldwide idea of extravagance markets expects brands to explore the social subtleties of their main interest groups. Extravagance is certainly not a one-size-fits-all idea; a dynamic and versatile peculiarity takes on various structures and implications in different social settings.

All in all, the meaning of extravagance is a liquid and dynamic idea that envelops a wide range of encounters, items, and ways of life. It is a sign of eliteness, extraordinary quality, and the quest for joy. From unmistakable belongings to elusive encounters, from the rarities of craftsmanship to the advantage of time, the features of extravagance are different and consistently advancing. As society advances, so too will the forms of extravagance, molded by social movements, innovative headways, and the changing goals of people looking to hoist their lives through the quest for richness.

1.3 Evolution of Luxury in History

The development of extravagance in history is a charming excursion that winds through the texture of human civilization, mirroring the changing elements of social orders, societies, and people. Extravagance, in its different structures, has existed since old times, arising as a marker of riches, influence, and refinement. As we follow the verifiable direction of extravagance, we reveal a story that rises above simple material belongings, including a rich embroidery of workmanship, craftsmanship, encounters, and cultural qualities.

Old developments like Mesopotamia, Egypt, and Rome give early looks into the underlying foundations of extravagance. In these social orders, the exclusive class exhibited their fortune through lavish belongings and extreme ways of life. Valuable metals, gemstones, and finely created antiquities represented status and were frequently utilized as presentations of abundance and power. The shortage of these materials and the work serious cycles associated with their creation made them selective images of extravagance.

In the antiquated world, extravagance was firmly entwined with the idea of obvious utilization. The more extravagant and uncommon the belongings, the more noteworthy the distinction they gave upon their proprietors. Elaborate meals, flashy apparel, and finely enhanced homes were not only articulations of solace however explanations of social standing. The accessibility of extravagance products was an indication of thriving, and the craving for eliteness was profoundly implanted in the human mind.

The Silk Street, the old exchange network interfacing East and West, assumed a critical part in the trading of extravagance merchandise and social impacts. Flavors, silks, valuable stones, and other fascinating products crossed huge distances, making a worldwide commercial center for extravagance things. The Silk Street worked with monetary trades as well as filled in as a conductor for the spread of creative and mechanical progressions, adding to the development of extravagance.

The Medieval times saw the ascent of primitive social orders, where the nobility held tremendous power and controlled admittance to assets. Extravagance, in this time, was frequently inseparable from primitive honor. Palaces and fabulous homes enhanced with embroidered works of art, resplendent furnishings, and intriguing fine arts became images of respectable riches. The primitive master's way of life, portrayed by dining experiences, diversion, and extreme attire, set the norm for extravagance in middle age Europe.

The Renaissance denoted a groundbreaking period in the development of extravagance, introducing a recovery of old style workmanship, writing, and reasoning. The rich trader class, enabled by monetary achievement, started to challenge the strength of the nobility.

The Renaissance first class embraced a more humanistic way to deal with life, appreciating the excellence of human expression and the quest for information. Extravagance during this period reached out past material belongings to incorporate social refinement, training, and the support of artistic expression.

The Period of Investigation in the fifteenth and sixteenth hundreds of years extended the skylines of extravagance by presenting new and fascinating merchandise from far off lands. The convergence of flavors, valuable metals, and materials from Asia, Africa, and the Americas improved the material scene of Europe. The thriving shipping lanes and the foundation of pioneer domains added to the making of a worldwide extravagance market, where the obtaining of interesting and intriguing things turned into an image of social distinction.

The eighteenth century saw the development of the Edification, a period described by scholarly interest, logical request, and a reconsideration of cultural standards. The idea of extravagance went through a change as Illumination scholars addressed customary orders and upheld for individual privileges and opportunities. The ascent of the working class, powered by industrialization and financial development, prompted a democratization of extravagance, making once-selective merchandise more open to a more extensive portion of society.

The Modern Upheaval in the nineteenth century further sped up changes in the extravagance scene. Large scale manufacturing procedures changed assembling processes, making extravagance things more reasonable and accessible to a more extensive crowd. While customary craftsmanship endured, the coming of plants and the motorization of creation considered the replication of extravagance merchandise on a scale beforehand impossible. The charm of extravagance was not generally bound to the gentry; it turned into an optimistic pursuit for the prospering working class.

The Beauty Époque period of the late nineteenth and mid twentieth hundreds of years denoted a re-visitation of extravagance and polish. The monetary thriving of the time, especially in Europe and North America, powered a reestablished interest in extravagance living. The more elite classes of society enjoyed luxurious ways of life, decorated with resplendent style, rich gatherings, and excellent bequests. Workmanship and culture prospered, with the cutting edge developments pushing the limits of innovativeness and rethinking ideas of extravagance feel.

The repercussions of The Second Great War and the monetary difficulties of the interwar period provoked a change in the view of extravagance.

The Thundering Twenties, described by friendly disturbance and social dynamism, saw the development of another type of extravagance that embraced innovation and a freed way of life. Workmanship Deco, with its striking mathematical plans and lavish materials, turned into the visual articulation of this time. The quest for delight, recreation, and gluttonous extravagance became focal topics in the advancing account of extravagance.

The Second Great War and its consequence achieved a time of somberness, impacting the definition and utilization of extravagance. Scant assets and an emphasis on remaking social orders incited a reconsideration of over the top plushness. The post-war period saw a shift towards downplayed class and a longing for legitimacy in extravagance. The accentuation on craftsmanship, quality, and getting through esteem acquired conspicuousness as shoppers looked for ageless pieces over short lived patterns.

The last 50% of the twentieth century saw the democratization of extravagance arrive at new levels. The ascent of commercialization, powered by publicizing, media, and the worldwide economy, added to a culture where the ownership of extravagance things became inseparable from progress and status. Originator names, extravagance style houses, and notable brands became images of optimistic residing, rising above financial limits.

The late twentieth century likewise saw a developing familiarity with social and natural issues, inciting a shift towards more dependable and economical extravagance rehearses. The craving for realness stretched out past the actual item to incorporate the moral and natural contemplations related with its creation. Extravagance buyers started to look for brands that lined up with their qualities, introducing a period of cognizant utilization inside the extravagance market.

The 21st century achieved extraordinary changes in the extravagance scene, molded by mechanical headways, globalization, and advancing customer inclinations. The advanced upset and the ascent of internet business changed how extravagance products were showcased, sold, and consumed. Web-based entertainment stages became persuasive features for lavish ways of life, empowering brands to interface straightforwardly with buyers and make vivid advanced encounters.

The idea of experiential extravagance acquired conspicuousness in the 21st hundred years, mirroring a change in customer needs towards encounters over belongings. Extravagance voyagers looked for exceptional and vivid excursions, culinary lovers sought after selective eating encounters, and health turned into a point of convergence of extravagance living. The immaterial parts of extravagance, like customized administration, social improvement, and close to home reverberation, started to offset the significance of material belongings.

Mechanical development additionally tracked down its direction into the universe of extravagance, with savvy innovation and customization becoming necessary to the advanced extravagance experience. From brilliant homes with robotized frameworks to customized items custom-made to individual inclinations, innovation consistently coordinated into the lavish way of life. The crossing point of extravagance and innovation made additional opportunities for customization, personalization, and upgraded accommodation.

The development of extravagance in history mirrors a unique transaction of monetary, social, and cultural powers. From the richness of antiquated civilizations to the democratization of extravagance in the advanced time, the meaning of extravagance has ceaselessly developed, adjusting to the changing qualities and goals of social orders. Today, extravagance isn't only about having costly things; a comprehensive idea includes validness, experience, and a feeling of prosperity. As we explore the intricacies of the 21st hundred years, the direction of extravagance keeps on being formed by a juncture of worldwide impacts, mechanical progressions, and a redefinition of living a really sumptuous life.

1.4 Significance of Five-Star Excellence

The meaning of five-star greatness rises above the domain of simple convenience; it typifies a pledge to unmatched help, refined encounters, and a steady devotion to the specialty of cordiality. A five-star foundation isn't simply a spot to remain; it is a safe-haven of extravagance, where everything about organized to lift the visitor experience to remarkable levels. In investigating the meaning of five-star greatness, we dig into the multi-layered components that add to its conspicuousness in the realm of extravagance neighborliness.

Key to the meaning of five-star greatness is the firm obligation to support. Each cooperation, from the second a visitor shows up to takeoff time, is fastidiously coordinated to surpass assumptions. The assistance faculty, prepared to expect the requirements and wants of the insightful visitor, become representatives of extravagance, encapsulating the ethos of friendliness. The customized consideration and consistent execution of each and every help establish a climate where the visitor feels obliged as well as really focused on.

The quest for greatness is manifest in the engineering plan of five-star foundations. These designs go past simple usefulness, filling in as masterpieces that spellbind the faculties and make a prompt feeling of wonderment. Pretentious entryways, embellished with lavish goods and engineering wonders, set the vibe for the rich experience that exists in.

The meaning of the actual space isn't just about giving safe house; about establishing a vivid climate reverberates with plushness and complexity.

The visitor rooms inside a five-star foundation are safe-havens of solace and refinement. The importance lies not just in the extravagant goods and rich conveniences yet in addition in the fastidious tender loving care. From the choice of premium materials to the nicely organized stylistic layout, every component adds to an agreeable feel that encompasses the visitor in a case of extravagance. The engineering and plan of the rooms are painstakingly created to give a feeling of quietness and break from the conventional.

Culinary greatness is a foundation of the five-star insight. The meaning of gastronomy inside these foundations reaches out past simple food; it turns into an excursion of the faculties. From Michelin-featured cafés to hint bistros, the culinary contributions are a demonstration of the devotion to quality and development.

Magnificent cooks curate menus that exhibit a combination of flavors, using the best fixings to make paramount feasting encounters. The meaning of culinary greatness lies in its capacity to hoist the general visitor experience, making each feast a festival of extravagance.

The spa and health offices inside five-star foundations contribute fundamentally to the comprehensive prosperity of the visitors. These safe-havens of unwinding are intended to give a rest from the burdens of present day life. The meaning of wellbeing inside the extravagance experience lies in the joining of customary strategies and state of the art medicines to sustain the body, psyche, and soul. Spa withdraws become safe houses of restoration, offering a scope of administrations that mirror a guarantee to comprehensive wellbeing and a significant comprehension of the meaning of prosperity.

The meaning of five-star greatness stretches out past the singular visitor to take special care of the requirements of corporate clients. The meeting and occasion offices inside these foundations are furnished with cutting edge innovation and deal a degree of administration that befits significant level discussions and vital get-togethers. The importance lies in giving a scene as well as in establishing a climate helpful for efficiency and consistent execution. Business voyagers find a safe house where extravagance flawlessly coordinates with usefulness.

The appeal of five-star greatness isn't restricted to a specific geological area or social milieu. A worldwide peculiarity rises above borders and social contrasts. The meaning of these foundations lies in their capacity to give a predictable norm of greatness while embracing the novel qualities of their regions. Whether settled in the core of an energetic city, roosted on a peaceful waterfront retreat, or encompassed by the quietness of nature, every five-star foundation offers a particular yet generally sumptuous experience.

Innovation assumes a huge part in molding the visitor experience inside five-star foundations. The meaning of mechanical reconciliation goes past simple comfort; it turns into a device for upgrading personalization and customization. From brilliant room controls to intuitive attendant services, innovation is consistently woven into the texture of extravagance accommodation. The importance lies in its capacity to offer a harmony between state of the art development and the immortal practices of administration.

The natural awareness that has penetrated the advanced time tracks down articulation in the maintainability drives inside five-star foundations. The meaning of eco-accommodating practices, from green structure plans to mindful obtaining of materials, mirrors a promise to moral stewardship of the planet. Extravagance, once inseparable from overabundance, is developing to embrace a more mindful and reasonable ethos. The meaning of this shift isn't simply in fulfilling the needs of socially cognizant voyagers yet in setting a norm for the eventual fate of lavish living.

The meaning of five-star greatness lies in its versatility to the changing scene of extravagance. As cultural qualities advance, so too does the meaning of plushness. The capacity of these foundations to embrace arising patterns, take care of moving inclinations, and remain on the ball is a demonstration of their persevering through importance. From the lavishness of the past to the supportable extravagance representing things to come, five-star greatness stays at the very front of the always developing story of guilty pleasure.

In a time where experiential extravagance is acquiring noticeable quality, the meaning of making minutes and recollections becomes vital. Five-star greatness goes past offering a support; it is tied in with creating encounters that resound with the visitor on an individual level. Whether it's an arranged culinary excursion, a select health retreat, or a custom tailored social drenching, the importance lies in the capacity to make recollections that wait long after the visitor has left the premises.

The meaning of five-star greatness reaches out to its job as a social powerhouse. These foundations frequently become famous milestones that add to the character and picture of an objective. The social importance lies in the building wonders as well as in the effect they have on the nearby economy, the travel industry, and the general view of the district. Five-star greatness turns into a signal that draws in guests, financial backers, and forces to be reckoned with, forming the story of a district.

All in all, the meaning of five-star greatness in the domain of extravagance friendliness is complex and persevering. It goes past the lavishness of facilities to include a guarantee to support, a hug of wellbeing, a festival of culinary expressions, and a mix of innovation. These foundations become something other than spots to remain; they are vivid conditions that weave a story of extravagance. The importance lies not just in measuring up to the assumptions of the insightful visitor yet in surpassing them, making an encounter that waits in the memory as a benchmark of lavish living. As the universe of extravagance keeps on developing, the meaning of five-star greatness stays a directing light, making way for the following part in the story of unrivaled neighborliness.

Chapter 2

The Art of Hospitality

The specialty of friendliness is a complex idea that reaches out past the simple arrangement of convenience or administrations. It incorporates a significant comprehension of human association, social subtleties, and the fragile dance of expecting and satisfying the necessities of visitors. In a world that is progressively interconnected, the significance of neighborliness couldn't possibly be more significant. Whether it's the warm greeting stretched out to an exhausted explorer, the fastidious scrupulousness in a top notch food experience, or the consistent association of occasions, the specialty of cordiality winds around its enchantment through different features of life.

At its center, cordiality is tied in with making a feeling of having a place and solace for people who are away from their natural environmental factors. This feeling is typified in the immortal precept, "mi casa es su casa," meaning "my home is your home." It addresses the quintessence of neighborliness — an encouragement to share and participate in the liberality of a host. This basic yet significant motion encapsulates the soul that underlies all demonstrations of friendliness — the ability to cause others to feel comfortable, to facilitate their excursion, and to advance their encounters.

The underlying foundations of cordiality follow back to antiquated times when the idea of visitor companionship, or xenia, held extraordinary importance in Greek culture. This consecrated practice included the trading of favors among hosts and visitors, cultivating a security that rose above simple exchanges. The visitor was treated as a heavenly emissary, and the host was compelled by a sense of honor to offer security, food, and diversion. This proportional relationship went past the material domain;

it was an affirmation of shared humankind and the interconnectedness of individuals.

As social orders advanced, so did the statements of friendliness. In middle age Europe, the idea of the motel arose as an imperative component of the friendliness scene. Motels gave a spot to rest as well as a collective space where explorers could share stories, trade news, and fashion associations. The owner, frequently a focal figure locally, assumed a urgent part in organizing these communications, making a microcosm of the bigger world inside the bounds of the motel.

The Renaissance time frame saw the ascent of excellent royal residences and châteaux, where friendliness turned into a show of plushness and refinement. Rich dinners and excessive stimulations were organized to exhibit the abundance and social complexity of the host.

The accentuation on feel and the quest for joy laid the preparation for the development of friendliness as a work of art — a fragile harmony between the substantial and the elusive, the useful and the tasteful.

In the cutting edge time, the neighborliness business has blossomed into a worldwide behemoth, enveloping lodgings, eateries, travel services, and a horde of different administrations. The standards of neighborliness, be that as it may, remain well established in the basic upsides of warmth, liberality, and mindfulness. Whether it's a shop lodging in a cosmopolitan city or a family-possessed café in a curious town, the craft of friendliness pervades the environment, molding the general insight for visitors.

Integral to the specialty of accommodation is the idea of expectation — the capacity to perceive and satisfy the necessities of visitors before they articulate them. This natural comprehension goes past simple proficiency; it includes a profound sympathy that permits hosts to make a consistent and customized insight. From expecting dietary inclinations to giving insightful conveniences, the specialty of friendliness relies on the capacity to surpass assumptions and have a permanent effect on visitors.

Social capability is one more pivotal feature of neighborliness. As the world turns out to be progressively interconnected, has should explore the subtleties of different societies to establish a comprehensive and inviting climate. This goes past superficial signals and stretches out to a veritable appreciation and regard for the traditions, customs, and responsive qualities of visitors from various foundations. The specialty of friendliness, thusly, includes a ceaseless course of learning and transformation to guarantee that each visitor feels seen, esteemed, and regarded.

The actual space wherein friendliness unfurls assumes a critical part in forming the general insight. Whether it's the plan of a lodging entryway, the format of an eatery, or the vibe of an occasion scene, the feel and usefulness of the space add to the story of friendliness. Insightful plan can bring out feelings, invigorate discussion, and make an enduring impression. The specialty of cordiality stretches out to the fastidious curation of everything about, the variety range to the decision of furniture, fully intent on making a tangible excursion for the visitors.

Inside the domain of neighborliness, culinary expressions stand apart as a particular and strong articulation of inventiveness. Food can bring out recollections, trigger feelings, and make a feeling of association. A professional dinner isn't simply a wellspring of food; it is a type of narrating, with each dish portraying a story of fixings, strategies, and social impacts. The culinary expert, as a narrator, turns into a significant figure in the friendliness story, deciphering enthusiasm and development onto the plate.

In the realm of top notch food, the idea of a tasting menu has acquired conspicuousness as a vehicle for culinary narrating. This cautiously arranged venture through numerous courses permits gourmet experts to feature their abilities, inventiveness, and the variety of flavors.

The craft of neighborliness in top notch food reaches out past the culinary domain; it envelops the movement of administration, the determination of flatware, and the organization of the whole feasting experience. Every component is painstakingly adjusted to make an agreeable orchestra that resounds with the faculties.

The drink business, as well, assumes a critical part in the embroidery of cordiality. From sommeliers directing visitors through a wine matching encounter to mixologists creating custom mixed drinks, the specialty of refreshment administration adds a layer of refinement and joy to the general cordiality experience. The exchange between flavors, fragrances, and show adds to the tangible excursion, raising the visitor's view of the foundation.

The computerized age has introduced another aspect to the craft of friendliness. Online stages and web-based entertainment act as useful assets for correspondence and advertising, molding the view of neighborliness foundations. The virtual domain, be that as it may, can't supplant the substantial parts of human association and actual experience. The test for friendliness experts in the computerized period is to work out some kind of harmony between utilizing innovation for effectiveness and saving the genuineness of individual connections.

In the contemporary scene, manageability has turned into a vital thought in the specialty of accommodation. As natural cognizance develops, visitors progressively look for foundations that line up with their upsides of eco-benevolence and social obligation. Cordiality experts are adjusting by integrating feasible practices, from energy-proficient plan to privately obtained fixings. The specialty of friendliness, in this specific situation, includes a promise to moral and capable strategic policies that add to the prosperity of the two visitors and the planet.

Occasions and festivities give one more material to the specialty of accommodation to unfurl. Whether it's a wedding, a corporate get-together, or a social celebration, the outcome of an occasion depends on the consistent coordination of horde subtleties. Occasion organizers, likened to guides, coordinate different components to make a strong and noteworthy experience. The craft of friendliness in occasions lies in the capacity to wind around a story that resounds with the subject, reason, and desires of the event.

Past the business domain, the craft of neighborliness tracks down articulation in the domain of medical care. Patient-focused care puts the person at the core of the clinical experience, perceiving the significance of compassion, correspondence, and solace in the mending system. The clinic climate, customarily somber and clinical, is developing to embrace standards of neighborliness to make a seriously inviting and strong space for patients and their families.

Training, as well, isn't absolved from the impact of cordiality. The shift from conventional study halls to experiential learning conditions mirrors a comprehension of the effect of room and air on the learning venture.

Instructive organizations that focus on cordiality in their methodology encourage a feeling of local area, coordinated effort, and commitment among understudies, establishing a climate helpful for comprehensive turn of events.

The specialty of accommodation isn't restricted to formal settings; it pervades regular connections and signals. A comforting grin from a more peculiar, some assistance in the midst of hardship, or a basic thoughtful gesture — every one of these comprise microcosmic articulations of friendliness. In a world that can once in a while appear to be cold and uninterested, these little demonstrations act as tokens of our common mankind and the potential for positive associations.

The idea of the "third spot" acquaints one more aspect with the craft of neighborliness. Authored by humanist Beam Oldenburg, the term alludes to spaces past the home (in front of the rest of the competition) and the work environment (second spot) where individuals accumulate for social connection. Bistros, public venues, and recreational areas are instances of third places that cultivate a feeling of having a place and local area. The craft of neighborliness in these spaces lies in the formation of a climate that energizes mingling, coordinated effort, and the trading of thoughts.

2.1 The Foundation of Five-Star Service

The groundwork of five-star administration is a bedrock of greatness, accuracy, and an unflinching obligation to surpassing assumptions. A complex methodology goes past simple exchanges, intending to make a vivid and remarkable experience for visitors. Established in the standards of friendliness, the underpinning of five-star administration is a fragile harmony between expecting the requirements of visitors and conveying a degree of administration that is completely excellent.

At the center of five-star administration is the rule of customized consideration. Dissimilar to normalized administration models, five-star administration perceives the uniqueness of every visitor and tries to fit the experience to their singular inclinations. This requires a profound comprehension of the specialty of expectation — an expertise that permits specialist organizations to meet as well as outperform the assumptions for visitors before those assumptions are even expressed.

Expectation in five-star administration includes a degree of instinct that goes past the value-based parts of neighborliness. It requires administration experts to peruse unpretentious prompts, figure out implicit inclinations, and make a consistent encounter that feels tailor-made for every visitor. This capacity to expect needs is the sign of genuinely extraordinary help and is many times what recognizes a five-star insight from a more standard help offering.

The scrupulousness in five-star administration is careful and reaches out to each part of the visitor experience. From the second a visitor enters a five-star foundation, they ought to feel wrapped in an environment of extravagance, solace, and care. The actual space, the plan components, and, surprisingly, the selection of decorations all assume a part in making a vibe that is helpful for unwinding and satisfaction.

In the domain of five-star lodgings, the scrupulousness is apparent in the plan of the hall, the nature of materials utilized, and the consistent combination of innovation. The objective is to establish a climate that isn't just tastefully satisfying yet additionally useful and helpful for the necessities of the visitors. Each component is organized with accuracy, from the work of art on the walls to the course of action of furniture, adding to a general feeling of extravagance and refinement.

The significance of certifiable cordiality couldn't possibly be more significant in that frame of mind of five-star administration. While the actual parts of the climate are essential, it is the glow and genuineness of the associations that hoist the experience to a higher level. The staff in a five-star foundation are not simply specialist organizations; they are envoys of friendliness, epitomizing the upsides of graciousness, sympathy, and a real craving to cause visitors to feel appreciated.

Preparing assumes a urgent part in guaranteeing that the staff is outfitted with the abilities and mentality vital for conveying five-star administration. From front-of-house work force to housekeeping staff, each colleague is an essential supporter of the general visitor experience. Preparing programs frequently center around specialized abilities as well as on delicate abilities like successful correspondence, the capacity to understand anyone on a profound level, and critical thinking.

In the domain of feasting, five-star administration stretches out to the culinary experience. The fastidious preparation and execution of a five-star dinner include the abilities of the gourmet specialists as well as the mastery of the help staff. From the choice of fixings to the introduction of dishes, each perspective is organized to make an ensemble of flavors that pleases the sense of taste. The help during a five-star feast is arranged with accuracy, with an accentuation on unpretentious yet mindful consideration.

The wine and refreshment administration in a five-star setting is a specific fine art. Sommeliers, frequently profoundly prepared specialists in their field, guide visitors through an organized choice of wines, guaranteeing that the matching upgrades the general eating experience. The meticulousness in the introduction of drinks, from the decision of dish sets to the pouring strategy, adds to the tangible excursion that characterizes five-star administration.

In the domain of extravagance travel, five-star administration reaches out past the limits of the lodging or eatery. It incorporates the whole visitor venture, from the snapshot of landing in the air terminal to the transportation to the inn and then some. Limousine administrations, individual attendant help, and organized encounters are all essential for the consistent embroidered artwork of administration that characterizes the zenith of accommodation.

The groundwork of five-star administration likewise lays on the standards of consistency and unwavering quality. Visitors anticipate a specific norm of greatness, and it is the obligation of the specialist organizations to reliably follow through on those assumptions. This requires a pledge to quality control, progressing preparing, and a culture of persistent improvement. A five-star foundation is one where visitors can believe that their experience will be reliably outstanding, no matter what the particular conditions of their visit.

Correspondence is a key part in the groundwork of five-star administration. Clear and open lines of correspondence between staff individuals, as well likewise with visitors, are fundamental for the smooth activity of any very good quality foundation. Successful correspondence guarantees that everybody is in total agreement, grasps the requirements and assumptions for the visitors, and can team up consistently to convey an impeccable encounter.

Flexibility is one more key part of the underpinning of five-star administration. While there are standard working methodology and conventions, the capacity to adjust to the one of a kind requirements and inclinations of every visitor is pivotal. This requires an adaptable outlook among staff individuals, a readiness to exceed all expectations to oblige unique solicitations, and the capacity to deal with startling difficulties with effortlessness and effectiveness.

The reconciliation of innovation is a cutting edge feature of the underpinning of five-star administration. While the human touch stays central, innovation can improve the visitor experience in different ways. Online reservation frameworks, versatile registrations, and customized applications that permit visitors to redo their experience are instances of how innovation can be consistently incorporated into the assistance model. Nonetheless, it's vital for find some kind of harmony, guaranteeing that innovation improves instead of cheapens the individual and human components of administration.

Security and protection are principal in the underpinning of five-star administration. High-profile visitors frequently pick five-star foundations for the confirmation of watchfulness and security. Hearty safety efforts, both noticeable and in the background, add to a feeling of trust and certainty among visitors. This incorporates secure access control, reconnaissance frameworks, and thoroughly prepared security faculty who work with a degree of tact that lines up with the ethos of five-star administration.

The groundwork of five-star administration isn't restricted to a particular industry or sort of foundation. Whether it's a lavish lodging, a fancy eatery, a spa, or a top of the line retail insight, the standards of five-star administration stay steady. The ongoing idea is a promise to greatness, a commitment to customized consideration, and a tireless quest for making snapshots of joy for visitors.

All in all, the groundwork of five-star administration is a blend of imaginativeness, accuracy, and a profound obligation to the prosperity and fulfillment of visitors. A way of thinking goes past the conditional idea of administration, trying to make a profound association and enduring recollections. From the tender loving care in the actual climate to the glow and truthfulness of communications, each component adds to the woven artwork of an encounter that is absolutely unprecedented. As the zenith of cordiality, five-star administration sets the norm for greatness, welcoming visitors into a reality where all their necessities isn't just met however surpassed with effortlessness and complexity.

2.2 Crafting Memorable Experiences

Making paramount encounters is a complicated craftsmanship that rises above the normal and changes minutes into enduring impressions. A multi-layered try requires a sharp comprehension of human feelings, a dominance of narrating, and a steady obligation to making something unprecedented. From the cordiality business to occasion arranging, promoting, and then some, the capacity to create paramount encounters has turned into a sign of outcome in a world that wants validness and association.

At the core of creating important encounters is the acknowledgment that an encounter is in excess of a grouping of occasions — it is a personal excursion. Whether it's a stay at a lavish inn, a visit to an amusement park, or cooperation in a corporate occasion, the close to home effect of the experience waits long after the unmistakable components disappear. Creating significant encounters includes purposefully planning these profound excursions to bring out good sentiments, manufacture associations, and leave an enduring engraving on the members.

The most common way of making paramount encounters frequently starts with a profound comprehension of the ideal interest group. Various people and socioeconomics have remarkable inclinations, wants, and responsive qualities. Creating an encounter that resounds requires a nuanced comprehension of the qualities, goals, and assumptions for the members. This includes statistical surveying, client profiling, and a pledge to remaining receptive to moving patterns and inclinations.

Narrating assumes a critical part in the specialty of making noteworthy encounters. Each experience has a story — a start, center, and end. The story shapes the members' discernments, directs their feelings, and weaves a durable string through the different components of the experience.

Whether it's the narrative of a brand, the story curve of an occasion, or the story told by the mood of a space, narrating imbues importance and reverberation into the general insight.

In the domain of friendliness, making vital encounters is inseparable from offering excellent support. Past the actual conveniences, the embodiment of a lavish inn or resort lies in the intangibles — the customized gladly received, the expectant help, and the certifiable consideration for the prosperity of visitors. The specialty of making vital encounters in cordiality is tied in with going past assumptions and making snapshots of joy that visitors will convey with them long after they leave.

In the realm of top notch food, making a vital culinary encounter includes something other than the flavors on the plate. It reaches out to the mood of the café, the introduction of the dishes, and the narrating behind each culinary creation. The gourmet expert turns into a narrator, and the feasting experience turns into a tactile excursion through preferences, smells, and surfaces. The coordination of administration, the determination of silverware, and, surprisingly, the plan of the menu add to the general account of the eating experience.

Occasion arranging is a space where the specialty of making critical encounters is raised higher than ever. Whether it's a wedding, a corporate gathering, or a live performance, the outcome of an occasion relies on the capacity to make minutes that reverberate with the members. Occasion organizers should think about everything about, the underlying greeting to the post-occasion follow-up, to guarantee a consistent and paramount experience. The coordinated factors, plan, and diversion components should adjust firmly to recount a convincing story.

Brands, as well, comprehend the force of making critical encounters for of building enduring associations with clients. From item dispatches to showcasing efforts, effective brands influence the profound effect of encounters to make brand devotion. The retail area, specifically, has seen a shift from value-based trades to experiential retail, where the actual store turns into a phase for vivid encounters that go past conventional shopping.

Innovation has opened up new outskirts in the specialty of making vital encounters. Computer generated reality (VR), expanded reality (AR), and intuitive advancements give instruments to make vivid and connecting with encounters. From virtual voyages through lodgings to intuitive shows in exhibition halls, innovation adds a layer of profundity to the general insight. Nonetheless, the test lies in coordinating innovation flawlessly, guaranteeing that it upgrades as opposed to occupies from the human and profound components of the experience.

Making paramount encounters likewise includes a promise to manageability and moral contemplations. As cultural qualities shift towards ecological cognizance and social obligation, members in encounters progressively look for realness and arrangement with their qualities. Reasonable practices, eco-accommodating drives, and a guarantee to moral obtaining add to the general story of an encounter, resounding with members who focus on these qualities.

In the domain of movement, the journey for extraordinary and credible encounters has brought about the peculiarity of experiential the travel industry. Voyagers look for something beyond an objective; they hunger for vivid and extraordinary encounters that permit them to interface with neighborhood societies and networks. The neighborliness business answers by organizing encounters that go past the regular vacation spots, offering a more profound and more significant commitment with the location.

The specialty of creating paramount encounters isn't restricted to excellent or extreme settings. Regular associations and little motions can likewise add to the production of enduring recollections. A veritable grin from a client support delegate, a manually written note from a brand, or a customized suggestion from a nearby aide — these little contacts have the ability to lift common minutes into phenomenal encounters. Along these lines, creating critical encounters turns into an ethos that pervades different parts of life.

Representative commitment and inward culture are fundamental to the method involved with creating important encounters. Bleeding edge staff, from client support agents to occasion coordinators, are the diplomats of the experience. Their commitment, energy, and obligation to greatness straightforwardly influence the nature of the experience for members. Associations that focus on representative prosperity, preparing, and a positive work culture are better situated to convey critical encounters.

The brain science of memory and feeling is a central thought in creating essential encounters. Studies have shown that feelings assume an essential part in memory development, and good feelings are bound to bring about paramount encounters. Planning encounters that inspire positive feelings — satisfaction, shock, stunningness — makes a more grounded engrave on members' recollections. This understanding illuminates the determination regarding varieties, music, and other tactile components that add to the profound scene of an encounter.

Making critical encounters likewise requires a component of hazard taking and development. The quest for the remarkable frequently includes venturing outside the safe place and testing traditional standards. Trial and error with novel ideas, intense plan decisions, and inventive ways to deal with commitment can separate an encounter from the ordinary. In any case, this development ought to be tempered with a profound comprehension of the crowd to guarantee reverberation and association.

Estimation and criticism components are urgent in the continuous course of making important encounters. Visitor criticism, surveys, and investigation give important bits of knowledge into the adequacy of an encounter. Ceaseless improvement in light of these experiences permits associations to refine their methodology, adjust to evolving inclinations, and remain on the ball. A guarantee to get-together and dissecting information guarantees that the specialty of making important encounters stays dynamic and responsive.

The idea of luck — a wonderful little treat or surprising revelation — adds a layer of sorcery to the specialty of creating essential encounters. While fastidious arranging is fundamental, leaving space for suddenness and fortunate minutes considers the making of genuinely exceptional and credible encounters. These surprising joys, whether an opportunity experience, a spontaneous occasion, or an unexpected contort, add to the wealth of the general insight.

All in all, making noteworthy encounters is a craftsmanship that winds around together imagination, brain science, and a profound comprehension of human association. A way of thinking stretches out past unambiguous businesses or areas, contacting each feature of life where human encounters unfurl. Whether it's the greatness of a lavish lodging, the closeness of an eating experience, the energy of an occasion, or the regular connections with a brand, the capacity to create vital encounters is a sign of greatness. A workmanship changes the everyday into the remarkable, making minutes that resound, wait, and become treasured recollections. As people, associations, and social orders keep on looking for importance and association, the art of making vital encounters remains as a guide, welcoming us to raise the normal and embrace the unprecedented.

2.3 Importance of Personalization

The significance of personalization in the present dynamic and interconnected world couldn't possibly be more significant. As people, shoppers, and members in different parts of life, we progressively look for encounters that resound with our one of a kind inclinations, requirements, and desires. Personalization, in its different structures, has turned into a foundation in areas going from promoting and client support to medical care, training, and then some. It is an amazing asset that improves client fulfillment as well as encourages a more profound feeling of association and commitment.

In the domain of showcasing, personalization has developed from an original idea to a fundamental procedure for brands trying to slice through the commotion of a soaked market. The period of one-size-fits-all promoting is giving approach to designated and customized crusades that talk straightforwardly to the person. Propels in information examination, computerized reasoning, and AI empower brands to accumulate and break down huge measures of information, permitting them to grasp their crowd on a granular level.

One of the most apparent signs of customized advertising is in the domain of web based business. Online retailers influence information examination to follow client conduct, inclinations, and buy history. This data is then used to give customized proposals, custom-made advancements, and a consistent shopping experience. From recommending items in view of past buys to offering select limits on things of interest, web based business stages are at the bleeding edge of the personalization transformation.

Email promoting is another space where personalization assumes a urgent part. Gone are the times of nonexclusive mass messages shipped off whole mailing records. Today, email crusades are finely tuned to individual inclinations, with customized titles, content, and offers. Brands that put resources into figuring out their clients and conveying customized email content are bound to catch consideration, encourage brand devotion, and drive transformations.

In the realm of virtual entertainment, personalization is implanted in calculations that curate content in light of client communications, inclinations, and past way of behaving. Stages like Facebook, Instagram, and TikTok influence refined calculations to give clients a customized channel, exhibiting content that lines up with their inclinations and commitment designs. This customized content conveyance keeps clients connected as well as fills in as an amazing asset for publicists to target explicit socioeconomics with accuracy.

The meaning of personalization reaches out past advertising and pervades the domain of client care. In a period where client experience is a vital differentiator for brands, the capacity to offer customized and responsive support is central. Client support stages influence information to expect client needs, customize cooperations, and resolve issues productively. Whether it's a chatbot that comprehends regular language, a help specialist furnished with point by point client profiles, or mechanized frameworks that recollect past cooperations, personalization is the key part of remarkable client support.

The medical care industry is going through a change driven, to a limited extent, by the significance of personalization. Customized medication, which tailors clinical treatment to individual qualities, has arisen as a weighty way to deal with medical care. Progresses in genomics, sub-atomic diagnostics, and information examination empower medical services experts to grasp the extraordinary hereditary cosmetics of patients. This information takes into account more exact analysis, treatment arranging, and prescription determination, limiting aftereffects and improving results.

The shift towards patient-driven care is one more appearance of the significance of personalization in medical services. Rather than a one-size-fits-all methodology, medical care suppliers progressively perceive the benefit of grasping patients as the need might arise, inclinations, and conditions. Customized care plans, correspondence systems, and treatment regimens add to a more comprehensive and viable medical services insight.

In the domain of schooling, personalization is changing conventional models of learning. Versatile learning stages use information and investigation to fit instructive substance to the singular requirements and learning styles of understudies. This approach perceives that every student is one of a kind, with various qualities, shortcomings, and speeds of learning. Customized growth opportunities upgrade understanding as well as cultivate a really captivating and pleasant instructive excursion.

In the working environment, the significance of personalization is reflected in the developing accentuation on representative experience. Ground breaking associations grasp that a customized way to deal with representative commitment, improvement, and prosperity adds to higher work fulfillment, efficiency, and maintenance. Customized vocation improvement plans, adaptable work courses of action, and acknowledgment programs custom-made to individual inclinations are instances of how associations focus on the remarkable requirements of their labor force.

The ascent of personalization in different areas isn't without its difficulties and contemplations. Security concerns pose a potential threat as the assortment and utilization of individual information become more pervasive. Finding some kind of harmony among personalization and protection is a fragile dance that requires straightforwardness, assent, and hearty safety efforts. Associations that focus on moral information rehearses construct entrust with their clients, encouraging a positive relationship that goes past the value-based.

The significance of personalization isn't restricted to the computerized domain; it stretches out to the actual spaces we possess. Savvy homes, outfitted with customized environment control, lighting, and theater setups, represent the incorporation of personalization into our residing spaces. The Web of Things (IoT) empowers gadgets to learn client inclinations and change settings as needs be, establishing a consistent and redid climate.

The social and media outlets have likewise embraced the significance of personalization. Web-based features, for instance, use calculations to suggest motion pictures, Programs, and music in light of individual survey and listening propensities. This customized content conveyance model takes care of the different preferences of clients, guaranteeing that they are given choices that line up with their inclinations.

The coming of virtual and increased reality advances further grows the conceivable outcomes of personalization. Virtual encounters can be redone to individual inclinations, permitting clients to drench themselves in conditions and stories that reverberate with their inclinations. From virtual travel encounters to customized virtual shows, these advances rethink the idea of custom-made and vivid substance.

The fate of personalization holds much more significant ramifications as innovations keep on progressing. The idea of the metaverse — a virtual common space that blends parts of web-based entertainment, internet gaming, increased reality, and computer generated reality — opens new outskirts for customized encounters. In the metaverse, people can make advanced symbols, participate in customized social communications, and investigate virtual spaces that mirror their inclinations and personalities.

As we explore the developing scene of personalization, pondering its more extensive cultural impact is fundamental. On one hand, personalization upgrades comfort, proficiency, and client fulfillment. Then again, it brings up issues about the potential for channel bubbles, where people are simply presented to content and viewpoints that line up with their current convictions. Finding some kind of harmony that saddles the advantages of personalization while advancing variety, incorporation, and liberality is difficult for innovation engineers, policymakers, and society at large.

All in all, the significance of personalization is a principal trait of the contemporary human experience. From customized showcasing and client care to medical services, training, and then some, the capacity to fit encounters to individual inclinations is a strong power molding our connections with the world. As innovation proceeds to progress and our comprehension of personalization extends, the test lies in exploring the sensitive harmony among customization and security, guaranteeing that customized encounters enhance as opposed to restrict our points of view and associations. The excursion towards a more customized future is a dynamic and developing investigation of how innovation, information, and human yearnings cross in a world that undeniably esteems the uniqueness of every person.

2.4 Training the Exceptional Staff

Preparing extraordinary staff is a foundation of outcome in different enterprises, going from neighborliness and client care to medical services, schooling, and then some. The type of an association's staff straightforwardly influences the nature of administration, consumer loyalty, and by and large execution. Preparing, in this specific situation, isn't just a procedural activity however an essential interest in developing abilities, cultivating a positive work culture, and enabling people to succeed in their jobs.

In the neighborliness business, where the visitor experience is vital, the preparation of staff is a basic variable that can represent the moment of truth an inn or eatery's standing. Excellent staff preparing goes past showing fundamental work capabilities; it includes imparting a profound comprehension of the standards of friendliness, successful correspondence, and the specialty of expecting and surpassing visitor assumptions.

One critical part of preparing excellent staff in cordiality is underscoring the significance of the capacity to understand people on a deeper level. Friendliness experts are not simply specialist co-ops; they are diplomats of an encounter. Preparing programs frequently center around creating the capacity to understand people at their core abilities, empowering staff to explore different visitor collaborations with compassion, successful correspondence, and a sharp consciousness of non-verbal signs.

The idea of "administration with a grin" is more than a platitude; it mirrors the primary rule that a positive and inviting disposition is a key part of remarkable help. Preparing staff to really convey warmth and receptiveness makes an intriguing air for visitors.

This preparing reaches out to different jobs, from front-of-house staff to housekeeping, where each cooperation adds to the general visitor experience.

In the domain of client care, remarkable staff preparing is inseparable from outfitting delegates with the abilities to deal with a different scope of situations. This includes tending to routine requests and exchanges as well as exploring testing circumstances with amazing skill and critical thinking keenness. Successful client care preparing underlines undivided attention, compromise, and a pledge to surpassing client assumptions.

The preparation of extraordinary staff in medical services is a diverse undertaking that stretches out past the obtaining of specialized abilities. Medical services experts are depended with the prosperity of people, and their capacity to give humane and patient-focused care is fundamental. Preparing programs in medical services center around imparting a patient-first outlook, viable correspondence with patients and their families, and a pledge to moral and compassionate consideration.

In the schooling area, preparing excellent staff is vital to establishing a positive and improving learning climate. Educators, managers, and care staff assume urgent parts in molding the instructive experience for understudies. Preparing programs center around educational methods, homeroom the executives, and procedures for encouraging a comprehensive and steady learning climate. The objective is to enable instructors to adjust to assorted learning styles and make significant instructive encounters.

In the corporate world, preparing extraordinary staff is essential to accomplishing hierarchical objectives and keeping an upper hand. Proficient improvement programs cover a scope of abilities, from initiative and venture the board to viable correspondence and joint effort. These projects plan to develop a labor force that isn't just capable in their particular jobs yet in addition versatile to developing industry patterns and difficulties.

The preparation of outstanding staff reaches out to the improvement of administration abilities. Powerful initiative is an impetus for hierarchical achievement, impacting group elements, representative commitment, and by and large efficiency. Initiative preparation programs center around improving abilities, for example, essential reasoning, navigation, and the capacity to rouse and propel groups. Outstanding pioneers set the vibe for a positive work culture and add to the general achievement and development of an association.

The significance of constant learning in staff preparing couldn't possibly be more significant. In quickly developing ventures and dynamic workplaces, keeping up to date with new advances, best practices, and industry patterns is fundamental. Associations that focus on a culture of consistent learning make a labor force that is versatile, creative, and tough notwithstanding change.

Compelling staff preparing is certainly not a one-size-fits-all undertaking; it requires a custom-made approach that thinks about the interesting necessities and objectives of the association. Preparing projects ought to be lined up with the association's main goal, values, and long haul targets. This arrangement guarantees that staff preparing turns into an essential speculation that adds to the general achievement and supportability of the association.

Innovation has turned into a significant apparatus in the preparation of remarkable staff. E-learning stages, computer experiences, and intuitive preparation modules offer adaptable and versatile answers for associations, all things considered. These advancements empower staff to get to preparing materials at their own speed, partake in programmatic experiences to rehearse abilities, and participate in cooperative web based learning conditions.

The job of tutors and good examples is critical in the preparation of outstanding staff. Old pros who play succeeded in their parts can give important bits of knowledge, direction, and motivation to the people who are more current to the association. Mentorship programs encourage a culture of information sharing, joint effort, and ceaseless improvement, making a positive gradually expanding influence all through the association.

Delicate abilities, frequently alluded to as relational or relationship building abilities, are a critical concentration in the preparation of extraordinary staff. While specialized abilities are fundamental, the capacity to impart actually, team up with associates, and explore relational elements is similarly basic. Preparing programs that underscore the improvement of delicate abilities add to a positive work culture and upgrade by and large group viability.

Acknowledgment and prize components assume a crucial part in staff preparing. Excellent execution ought to be recognized and celebrated, encouraging a feeling of achievement and inspiration among staff. Acknowledgment can take different structures, from public affirmation of accomplishments to substantial rewards, for example, rewards or expert improvement valuable open doors. These systems add to a positive and persuading workplace.

With regards to staff preparing, variety, value, and incorporation (DEI) have arisen as fundamental contemplations. Preparing programs that focus on DEI go past superficial attention to address inclinations, encourage inclusivity, and advance a culture of regard and understanding. Staff preparing in DEI isn't just a reaction to cultural assumptions yet additionally an essential basic for associations planning to take advantage of different points of view and ability.

The assessment of staff preparing viability is a basic part of the general cycle. Associations ought to lay out clear measurements and key execution pointers (KPIs) to survey the effect of preparing programs. This assessment goes past conventional measures, for example, consummation rates and grades; it ought to incorporate input from staff, evaluations of genuine use of abilities, and an examination of the preparation's commitment to hierarchical objectives.

The significance of personalization in staff preparing has acquired noticeable quality. Perceiving that people have remarkable learning styles, inclinations, and qualities, customized preparing approaches improve commitment and maintenance. Preparing programs that offer adaptability in learning designs, consider independent learning ways, and consolidate certifiable situations custom-made to explicit jobs add to a more customized and successful preparation experience.

The coordination of innovation in staff preparing reaches out to the utilization of gamification. Gamified preparing modules influence components of game plan, like contest, rewards, and intelligent difficulties, to make learning seriously captivating and agreeable. Gamification upgrades the viability of preparing as well as encourages a feeling of energy and cordial contest among staff.

All in all, the preparation of extraordinary staff is a dynamic and key cycle that goes past the exchange of specialized abilities. It envelops the improvement of a positive work culture, the development of delicate abilities, and the strengthening of people to succeed in their jobs. From cordiality and medical services to schooling, corporate settings, and then some, associations that focus on remarkable staff preparing position themselves for outcome in a consistently developing and serious scene. As the labor force keeps on adjusting to new difficulties and valuable open doors, the obligation to progressing preparing and improvement turns into a critical differentiator for associations that try not exclusively to meet however to surpass assumptions.

Chapter 3

Architectural Splendor

Compositional quality is a term that epitomizes the glory, excellence, and development appeared in the plan and development of structures and designs since the beginning of time. It rises above simple usefulness, venturing into the domain of masterfulness and social articulation. Across civilizations and ages, planners have looked to make structures that fill viable needs as well as rouse stunningness and appreciation. This excursion through engineering quality takes us on a worldwide visit, investigating different styles, periods, and the development of design standards.

One of the earliest instances of compositional quality can be followed back to antiquated Egypt. The pyramids, especially the Incomparable Pyramid of Giza, stand as getting through images of human resourcefulness and designing ability. Developed a while back, these giant designs were worked as stupendous burial places for pharaohs, exhibiting a fastidious comprehension of math and galactic arrangement. The accuracy with which these pyramids were made remaining parts a demonstration of the high level information and craftsmanship of old Egyptian modelers.

Moving toward the west in time and topography, old Greece arises as one more pot of structural advancement. The Parthenon, roosted on the Acropolis in Athens, is a praiseworthy sign of old style Greek design. Developed in the fifth century BCE, this sanctuary committed to the goddess Athena is a superb mix of Doric sections, pediments, and friezes. The draftsmen, Ictinus and Callicrates, alongside the stone worker Phidias, made a construction that filled strict needs as well as typified the standards of congruity and extent vital to Greek feel.

Changing to the Roman Realm, the Pantheon in Rome remains as a demonstration of Roman designing ability and building development.

Underlying the second century CE, this sanctuary committed to every one of the divine beings includes a titanic vault with an oculus, or opening, at its summit. The Pantheon's vault, a wonder of substantial development, keeps on motivating engineers right up to the present day. The virtuoso of Roman planners lay in their capacity to push the limits of designing, making spaces that summon a feeling of loftiness and immortality.

As we navigate the archives of history, the building brilliant qualities of the Byzantine Domain call. Hagia Sophia, at first built as a house of prayer in Constantinople (cutting edge Istanbul), encapsulates Byzantine design.

Charged by Sovereign Justinian I in the sixth hundred years, Hagia Sophia's huge vault, many-sided mosaics, and creative utilization of pendentives exhibit the Byzantine planners' dominance in combining designing and style. The structure's change into a mosque during the Ottoman time adds one more layer to its rich history, mirroring the developing social embroidery of the locale.

The archaic period saw the ascent of Gothic engineering, portrayed by taking off basilicas that planned to arrive at the sky. Chartres Basilica in France is a quintessential model, with its sharp curves, ribbed vaults, and flying braces. Inherent the thirteenth hundred years, Chartres Basilica is a glorious articulation of the Gothic style, epitomizing a feeling of verticality and delicacy that recognizes it from prior structural structures. The developers' capacity to accomplish such accomplishments with the restricted mechanical assets of the time is a demonstration of their expertise and assurance.

The Renaissance denoted a recovery of old style impacts, introducing a recharged interest in extent, balance, and humanism. In Florence, Italy, Filippo Brunelleschi's vault for the Florence House of prayer remains as an unparalleled accomplishment of Renaissance engineering. Finished in the fifteenth hundred years, the vault exhibits Brunelleschi's imaginative utilization of a twofold shelled structure, shrewdly conveying the heaviness of the vault. This structural wonder represents the Renaissance soul as well as anticipates the logical and imaginative progressions of the next few centuries.

The Extravagant time frame that followed embraced show and richness in compositional plan. St. Peter's Basilica in Vatican City, planned by designers including Michelangelo and Gian Lorenzo Bernini, is a great representation of Ornate magnificence. The basilica's fabulous vault, transcending exterior, and luxurious inside make a feeling of drama that befits its status as an image of the Catholic Church's loftiness. The Ornate period's accentuation on feeling and scene made a permanent imprint on the engineering scene of Europe.

As we cross the Atlantic, the US unfurls a section of compositional quality with the coming of high rises in the late nineteenth and mid twentieth hundreds of years. The Chicago School of Design, drove by engineers, for example, Louis Sullivan and Daniel Burnham, spearheaded the advancement of tall structures with inventive steel-outline development. The Home Protection Building, finished in 1885, is viewed as the world's most memorable high rise, making way for the famous horizon of urban areas like Chicago and New York. High rises became images of American desire and financial ability, arriving at new levels both in a real sense and figuratively.

The twentieth century saw the development of present day design, testing conventional standards and embracing functionalism and moderation. The Bauhaus development, established by Walter Gropius in Germany, tried to coordinate workmanship, art, and innovation in structural plan.

The Bauhaus school's impact broadened around the world, with planners like Mies van der Rohe and Le Corbusier forming the innovator development. Le Corbusier's Manor Savoye, a worldview of the Worldwide Style, embodies the development's accentuation on clean lines, open spaces, and a dismissal of ornamentation.

Post-The Second Great War, another influx of design articulation arose with the coming of brutalism. Described by the utilization of crude concrete and strong, forcing structures, brutalist engineering planned to convey a feeling of solidarity and usefulness. The Public Auditorium in London, planned by Denys Lasdun and finished in 1976, is a notable brutalist structure that grandstands the development's sculptural and mathematical characteristics. While disruptive in popular assessment, brutalism has made a permanent imprint on the engineering scene, addressing a period of trial and error and idealistic beliefs.

At the same time, the late twentieth century saw a resurgence of interest in memorable protection and the consolidation of postmodern components in engineering. Postmodernism, supported by engineers like Robert Venturi and Denise Scott Brown, embraced mixture and a fun loving reevaluation of verifiable structures. The Piazza d'Italia in New Orleans, planned by Charles Moore, is a postmodern work of art that mixes traditional references with a feeling of eccentricity. This takeoff from the injuries of innovation permitted draftsmen to draw in with history while as yet pushing the limits of plan.

The 21st century has seen a continuation of structural variety and development, with a recharged center around supportability and mechanical reconciliation. The Burj Khalifa in Dubai, planned by Adrian Smith of the structural firm SOM, remains as the world's tallest structure, arriving at remarkable levels with its smooth plan and cutting edge designing.

As urban communities wrestle with issues of urbanization and natural effect, designers are progressively consolidating green structure practices and state of the art innovations to make structures that are both stylishly satisfying and biologically mindful.

The idea of starchitecture, where eminent planners are appointed to make famous designs, has additionally acquired unmistakable quality in the 21st hundred years. Straight to the point Gehry's Guggenheim Historical center Bilbao in Spain is a worldview of how design can turn into an impetus for metropolitan recharging and social renewal. The exhibition hall's undulating titanium-clad structures challenge show, making a dynamic and outwardly striking expansion to the Bilbao horizon. Starchitecture addresses a combination of imaginative vision and engineering development, changing urban communities and leaving an enduring engraving on their social character.

As we explore through the pages of engineering history, it becomes apparent that the thought of magnificence is intrinsically emotional, advancing with social, mechanical, and cultural movements.

Building magnificence isn't restricted to a particular style or period however is a continuum of inventiveness, answering the requirements and desires of every time. From the getting through pyramids of Egypt to the contemporary high rises of worldwide cities, the fabricated climate mirrors the aggregate creative mind and resourcefulness of mankind.

Additionally, the effect of design reaches out past the visual domain, impacting how we experience and interface with the spaces we possess. The plan of a structure can shape social elements, inspire profound reactions, and add to the social character of a local area. In this sense, designers are not just developers; they are narrators, winding around accounts through blocks and cement.

Notwithstanding feel and usefulness, planners today face the basic of maintainability. The ecological effect of development and the drawn out versatility of designs have become necessary contemplations in contemporary building practice. Green structure standards, sustainable power coordination, and eco-accommodating materials are currently fundamental parts of the designer's toolbox. This change in perspective mirrors a more extensive cultural consciousness of the interconnectedness between the constructed climate and the normal world.

Structural wonder likewise crosses with inquiries of social character and legacy conservation. The reclamation and versatile reuse of memorable structures have acquired unmistakable quality for the purpose of praising the past while tending to the necessities of the present. Versatile reuse projects, for example, changing over old processing plants into resident.

3.1 Designing Elegance

Planning tastefulness is a perplexing dance among structure and capability, feel and ease of use. A pursuit rises above simple ornamentation, diving into the substance of excellence and refinement in the making of spaces, items, and encounters. Whether in engineering, inside plan, design, or innovation, the journey for class requires a profound comprehension of equilibrium, concordance, and a careful scrupulousness.

In the domain of engineering, planning rich designs includes a sensitive transaction of lines, extents, and materials. The Parthenon, a zenith of traditional Greek engineering, epitomizes this quest for style. Built in the fifth century BCE on the Acropolis in Athens, the Parthenon's Doric segments, impeccably proportioned pediments, and multifaceted friezes add to a feeling of immortal magnificence. Building polish, in this unique circumstance, emerges from the agreeable coordination of components that fill a practical need as well as summon a feeling of elegance and refinement.

Pushing ahead in time, the Renaissance time frame saw a recharged interest in traditional standards and a festival of humanism. Planner Filippo Brunelleschi's plan for the Pazzi House of prayer in Florence, Italy, exemplifies the Renaissance journey for tastefulness.

Finished in the fifteenth hundred years, the church's straightforward mathematical structures, agreeable extents, and utilization of old style components grandstand Brunelleschi's dominance in making spaces that radiate a peaceful, downplayed magnificence. The Renaissance draftsmen tried to resuscitate the standards of old Greece and Rome, imbuing their plans with a feeling of equilibrium and extent that keeps on reverberating as the centuries progressed.

The Florid period, which followed the Renaissance, embraced a more fancy and dramatic way to deal with plan. In engineering, this appeared in vainglorious designs enhanced with intricate adornments and emotional lighting. The Castle of Versailles, worked during the seventeenth 100 years in France, under the heading of draftsmen like Jules Hardouin-Mansart, is a perfect representation of Rococo polish. The royal residence's lavish insides, unpredictable gardens, and overlaid subtleties mirror the period's propensity for abundance and luxury. While various in style from the Renaissance, the Ornate time frame shows one more feature of tastefulness — one that revels in the quality and wealth of plan.

The advancement of compositional polish went on into the eighteenth and nineteenth hundreds of years with the ascent of neoclassicism. Draftsman John Nash's work in Regime time London, especially the Illustrious Structure in Brighton, embodies neoclassical style. The Structure's combination of old style components with colorful subtleties makes a special and refined stylish. Neoclassicism, with its accentuation on evenness and traditional themes, looked to summon a feeling of request and pride. The polish in neoclassical plan lies in its capacity to reconsider old style structures while adjusting them to the preferences and upsides of the time.

As we progress into the twentieth 100 years, innovation arises as a prevailing compositional development, testing customary thoughts of polish. Modelers like Ludwig Mies van der Rohe and Le Corbusier supported a moderate methodology, inclining toward clean lines, open spaces, and a dismissal of ornamentation. Mies van der Rohe's Barcelona Structure, worked for the 1929 Global Piece, is a masterclass in pioneer class. The structure's utilization of materials like glass, steel, and marble makes a feeling of immaculateness and effortlessness, representing that tastefulness can be accomplished through a decrease of components to their fundamental structures.

In the last 50% of the twentieth 100 years, postmodernism arose as a response to the grimness of innovation. Postmodern draftsmen, for example, Robert Venturi and Michael Graves, embraced a more varied and energetic way to deal with plan. The Portland Working in Oregon, planned by Michael Graves and finished in 1982, is a postmodern milestone that challenges conventional ideas of polish. Its strong utilization of variety, noteworthy references, and lopsided sythesis challenge the pioneer standards of restriction, acquainting another aspect with the idea of class — one that is dynamic, various, and frequently provocative.

The 21st century introduced a reestablished center around maintainability and the reconciliation of state of the art advances in building plan. Eminent designers like Norman Encourage and Zaha Hadid have been at the front of this development, making structures that push the limits of development while keeping a feeling of tastefulness. Encourage's plan for the Swiss Re Building, ordinarily known as "The Gherkin," in London is a demonstration of this methodology. The structure's energy-productive highlights and particular, bended structure exhibit how tastefulness can coincide with ecological obligation and mechanical headway.

Inside plan, as a discipline, assumes a critical part in making conditions that exemplify style. The specialty of planning insides goes past simple design; it includes a smart thought of spatial game plans, variety ranges, and the choice of decorations. During the twentieth 100 years, inside planner Elsie de Wolfe spearheaded a more loose and reasonable way to deal with configuration, controlling away from the convention of past times. Her work, portrayed by an agreeable mix of solace and style, set up for another meaning of tastefulness — one that is congenial, individual, and intelligent of the occupants' ways of life.

The mid-century current development, with creators like Charles and Beam Eames, further underscored the reconciliation of structure and capability in inside spaces. The Eames Parlor Seat, a famous household item made in 1956, embodies the development's ethos of consolidating solace with creative plan. Its shaped compressed wood shell and cowhide upholstery give a happy with seating experience as well as add to a stylish that is immortal and easily stylish.

Contemporary inside plan keeps on developing, embracing a different scope of styles and impacts. The idea of "exquisite moderation" has acquired fame, with originators, for example, Axel Vervoordt embodying this methodology. Vervoordt's work frequently includes quieted variety ranges, normal materials, and an emphasis on making peaceful, cleaned up spaces. The class in this style emerges from the smart curation of components, permitting each detail to sparkle in its effortlessness.

In the domain of style, tastefulness is a consistently developing idea that rises above patterns and seasons. Coco Chanel, a trailblazer in twentieth century style, broadly expressed, "Tastefulness is refusal." Her plans, portrayed by clean lines and a dismissal of overabundance ornamentation, encapsulated another period of downplayed refinement. The little dark dress, an immortal creation by Chanel, turned into an image of rich straightforwardness that keeps on impacting style today.

Crafted by contemporary creators like Giorgio Armani and Phoebe Philo for Celine represents a cutting edge understanding of style in design. Armani's accentuation on fitting and a nonpartisan variety range makes a feeling of immortal refinement, while Philo's plans for Celine frequently embrace a moderate tasteful, commending the excellence of straightforwardness.

In the quick moving universe of style, where patterns go back and forth, these originators exhibit how getting through class can be accomplished through an emphasis on quality, craftsmanship, and an insightful alter of plan components.

Innovation, as well, has turned into a material for planning class in the cutting edge period. The smooth and moderate plan of Mac items, led by the late Steve Occupations and Boss Plan Official Jony Ive, embodies how innovation can be consistently coordinated into day to day existence with a bit of tastefulness. From the famous effortlessness of the iPhone to the accuracy designed MacBook, Mac's plan reasoning rotates around making items that are practical as well as tastefully satisfying.

The idea of planning class reaches out past substantial items to envelop client encounters in the advanced domain. UI (UI) and client experience (UX) planners assume a urgent part in making rich and natural connections. Organizations like Google, with its Material Plan standards, and

Airbnb, with its accentuation on a client driven approach, focus on effortlessness, clearness, and a consistent progression of communications to upgrade the general client experience.

All in all, planning class is a multi-layered try that unfurls across hundreds of years and disciplines. From the traditional evenness of old Greece to the moderate refinement of contemporary plan, the quest for style has taken on horde structures. Whether in engineering, inside plan, design, or innovation, the consistent idea lies in a fastidious tender loving care, a comprehension of equilibrium, and a pledge to establishing conditions, items, and encounters that rise above the normal.

Style isn't static; it develops with the moving sands of culture, innovation, and cultural qualities. It is an impression of our yearnings, a statement of our aggregate tasteful sensibilities. In every period, originators and engineers have wrestled with the test of characterizing and rethinking style, abandoning a tradition of immortal manifestations that proceed to rouse and enamor. As we explore the steadily changing scene of plan, the mission for style stays a core value — a compass that guides us toward an amicable association of magnificence and usefulness in the production of the world we occupy.

3.2 Iconic Structures and Interiors

Notorious designs and insides stand as demonstrations of human imagination, advancement, and the getting through journey for greatness in plan. These tourist spots, whether engineering wonders or dazzlingly planned spaces, become social images that rise above their actual presence, affecting the manner in which we see and experience our general surroundings. From old marvels to present day show-stoppers, these notorious designs and insides shape our aggregate personality and make a permanent imprint on the rich embroidered artwork of mankind's set of experiences.

One of the most prestigious compositional wonders of ancient times is the Incomparable Pyramid of Giza in Egypt. Developed a while back during the rule of Pharaoh Khufu, this pyramid is the biggest of the three pyramids on the Giza Level. The sheer scale and accuracy with which the Incomparable Pyramid was assembled keep on astounding researchers and engineers. Containing roughly 2.3 million limestone and rock hinders, each gauging a few tons, the pyramid's development stays an accomplishment that challenges how we might interpret old designing. Its impeccably adjusted sides and galactic importance have started speculations about its motivation and the high level information moved by the old Egyptians.

Pushing ahead in time, the Roman Colosseum remains as a persevering through image of old Rome's building and designing ability. Finished in

80 CE, this amphitheater could oblige up to 80,000 observers, facilitating gladiatorial challenges, creature chases, and public executions. The Colosseum's curved shape, layered seating, and complex arrangement of halls and chambers embody the Romans' dominance in planning huge, utilitarian spaces. Notwithstanding the desolates of time, the Colosseum stays a notorious design, drawing in large number of guests every year and filling in as a strong sign of Rome's social and verifiable heritage.

In the domain of strict design, Hagia Sophia in Istanbul, Turkey, remains as a demonstration of the building resourcefulness of the Byzantine Realm. Initially built as a church building in 537 CE under Sovereign Justinian I, Hagia Sophia later turned into a mosque during the Ottoman period and, all the more as of late, an exhibition hall. The structure's gigantic vault, mind boggling mosaics, and inventive utilization of pendentives feature the Byzantine modelers' capacity to make dazzling spaces that span the natural and the heavenly. Hagia Sophia's mind boggling history mirrors the social and strict movements that have molded the district throughout the long term.

Progressing to the Gothic period, the Notre-Woman Church in Paris remains as a model of French Gothic engineering. Development started in the twelfth 100 years, and the house of God's taking off towers, pointed curves, and perplexing stained glass windows convey a feeling of verticality and ethereal magnificence. The flying braces, a sign of Gothic plan, took into consideration the making of far reaching, light-filled insides. In spite of the overwhelming fire in 2019 that harmed bits of the house of God, Notre-Woman stays a getting through image of French social legacy and a demonstration of the craftsmanship of middle age manufacturers.

The Renaissance time frame saw the development of design jewels that commended traditional beliefs and humanism. The Vault of Florence Church building, planned by Filippo Brunelleschi in the fifteenth 100 years, remains as a magnum opus of Renaissance designing. Brunelleschi's creative twofold shelled vault, developed without the requirement for supporting wooden platform, denoted a defining moment in engineering history. The vault's elegant extents and amicable reconciliation with the basilica beneath mirror the Renaissance accentuation on numerical accuracy and a restoration of old style feel.

In the domain of private design, Honest Lloyd Wright's Fallingwater, finished in 1937, is a worldview of natural engineering that flawlessly coordinates with its normal environmental elements. Roosted over a cascade in country Pennsylvania, Fallingwater's cantilevered patios, even lines, and utilization of neighborhood materials exemplify Wright's way of thinking of planning structures together as one with nature. The house's imaginative plan obscures the limits among inside and outside, making a vivid and thoughtful residing space. Fallingwater stays a standard for planners investigating the connection between fabricated conditions and the normal world.

As the twentieth century unfurled, another influx of building development arose with the development of notable high rises. The Domain State Working in New York City, finished in 1931, turned into a seal of Craftsmanship Deco tastefulness and an image of American desire during the Economic crisis of the early 20s. Planned by designers William F. Sheep and Shreve, Sheep and Harmon, the structure's mishap plan, aluminum-clad tower, and taking off level made it the tallest structure on the planet at that point. The Realm Express Structure's persevering through prominence and social importance have set its place as quite possibly of the most notable construction in the advanced metropolitan scene.

In the last 50% of the twentieth hundred years, the Sydney Show House arose as a notable compositional accomplishment that reclassified the conceivable outcomes of structure and capability. Planned by Danish modeler Jørn Utzon and finished in 1973, the Show House's unmistakable sail-like shells make a striking outline against the Sydney Harbor. The structure's creative utilization of precast substantial boards and its reconciliation with the encompassing waterfront embody the soul of innovator trial and error. The Sydney Drama House has turned into a getting through image of Australia and an UNESCO World Legacy site, drawing in huge number of guests yearly.

The 21st century introduced another time of building articulation, set apart by mechanical progressions and a globalized plan language. The Burj Khalifa in Dubai, finished in 2010, remains as the world's tallest structure, arriving at a stunning level of 828 meters. Planned by the design firm SOM (Skidmore, Owings and Merrill), the Burj Khalifa's smooth profile, cutting edge designing, and intelligent glass exterior represent the fast turn of events and aspiration of the Assembled Bedouin Emirates. This notorious high rise fills in as a demonstration of the combination of state of the art innovation and structural plan on a worldwide scale.

All the while, the contemporary building scene highlights structures that focus on manageability and natural cognizance. The Bosco Verticale (Vertical Timberland) in Milan, planned by Stefano Boeri Architetti and finished in 2014, rethinks metropolitan living by integrating a large number of trees and plants into private pinnacles. The plant life gives an outwardly striking veneer as well as adds to further developed air quality and biodiversity. The Upward Backwoods represents a shift toward eco-cognizant engineering, where feel and manageability unite to make an agreeable connection between the fabricated climate and the regular world.

Notable insides, similar as their building partners, assume a significant part in molding our encounters and discernments. The Castle of Versailles, with its lavish Corridor of Mirrors, addresses the embodiment of Ornate inside plan. Brought about by planner Jules Hardouin-Mansart in the seventeenth hundred years, the Corridor of Mirrors highlights 357 mirrors, fancy overlaid moldings, and sweeping windows that mirror the encompassing nurseries. The space filled in as the setting for huge verifiable occasions, remembering the marking of the Settlement of Versailles for 1919, making it an image of political and social importance.

During the twentieth 100 years, the Farnsworth House by Ludwig Mies van der Rohe exhibited an extreme takeoff from conventional ideas of homegrown insides. Finished in 1951, this glass-walled home hazy spots the limits among indoor and outside spaces, offering unhindered perspectives on the encompassing scene. The Farnsworth House is a demonstration of Mies van der Rohe's moderate way of thinking, where straightforwardness and straightforwardness reclassify the idea of private class.

Contemporary inside plan frequently draws motivation from different impacts, with an accentuation on usefulness, solace, and an organized stylish. The inside of the Fondation Louis Vuitton in Paris, planned by planner Straightforward Gehry and finished in 2014, represents an agreeable mix of craftsmanship and design. The structure's liquid and straightforward design makes dynamic inside spaces that act as a scenery for contemporary workmanship displays. Gehry's utilization of glass and creative structures adds to a vivid and outwardly captivating experience inside the historical center's insides.

In the domain of cordiality plan, the Burj Al Middle Easterner in Dubai remains as an image of extravagance and plushness. Finished in 1999, this sail-molded lodging, planned by modeler Tom Wright, is eminent for its particular outline and rich insides. The utilization of rich materials, complex specifying, and all encompassing perspectives on the Bedouin Inlet add to the inn's standing as one of the world's most famous and extreme facilities. The Burj Al Bedouin's insides exhibit a combination of conventional Center Eastern themes with contemporary plan components, making a tangible encounter that mirrors the lodging's obligation to unmatched extravagance.

The idea of notable insides stretches out past actual spaces to incorporate articles that have become inseparable from plan greatness. The Eames Parlor Seat and Ottoman, made by Charles and Beam Eames in 1956, address a persevering through symbol of mid-century present day plan. The seat's shaped compressed wood shell, rich calfskin upholstery, and fastidiously designed subtleties embody the Eameses' obligation to frame and work. The Eames Parlor Seat has turned into an image of immortal class and a staple in plan assortments around the world.

In the domain of design, lead stores act as actual signs of a brand's personality and tasteful. The Chanel lead store on Lament Cambon in Paris, a space personally connected to the tradition of Coco Chanel, embodies the tastefulness and complexity inseparable from the brand. Planned by engineer Peter Marino, the store's inside consolidates current components with famous Chanel themes, making a sumptuous and vivid shopping experience. The interaction of light, surface, and materials mirrors the brand's obligation to making a space that lines up with its legacy while embracing contemporary plan sensibilities.

The plan of social establishments, like historical centers and theaters, additionally assumes a vital part in molding how we might interpret craftsmanship and cultivating social encounters. The Guggenheim Exhibition hall in Bilbao, Spain, planned by Straight to the point Gehry and finished in 1997, is a milestone that re-imagined the connection among design and social establishments. The historical center's undulating titanium-clad structures make a feeling of development and dynamism, filling in as a fitting setting for contemporary craftsmanship shows. The Guggenheim Bilbao's extraordinary effect on the city's social scene grandstands the capability of design to upgrade and fortify social organizations.

In the computerized age, the plan of virtual spaces has become progressively critical. The connection point and client experience plan of stages like Apple's iOS and Google's Material Plan for Android gadgets represent a promise to establishing instinctive and outwardly strong computerized conditions. These connection points focus on straightforwardness, lucidity, and a consistent progression of communications, mirroring a shift toward client driven plan in the innovation scene.

All in all, notorious designs and insides are more than actual elements — they are encapsulations of human resourcefulness, social qualities, and the advancing language of plan. From the old ponders that have endured everyday hardship to the contemporary show-stoppers that rethink our metropolitan scenes, these symbols shape our encounters and view of the constructed climate. The interchange of structure and capability, feel and utility, reverberations as the centuries progressed, leaving a permanent engraving on the aggregate memory of social orders all over the planet. As we keep on pushing the limits of plan, these notable designs and insides act as signals, directing us toward additional opportunities and rousing the up and coming age of draftsmen, architects, and pioneers.

3.3 Fusion of Tradition and Modernity

The combination of custom and innovation addresses a powerful interchange between the past and the present, a union of legacy and development that shapes the social scene of social orders all over the planet. This perplexing relationship appears across different spaces, from design and workmanship to mold and innovation, mirroring a continuum of human innovativeness and transformation. As customs develop notwithstanding current impacts, and innovation looks for motivation from verifiable roots, a rich embroidery of half and half articulations arises.

In the domain of engineering, the combination of custom and innovation frequently unfurls as a discourse between verifiable structures and contemporary plan standards. The Kyoto Worldwide Gathering Place in Japan fills in as an illustrative illustration of this unique cooperation. Finished in 1966 by engineer Sachio Otani, the meeting community consistently coordinates pioneer plan with conventional Japanese components. The structure's spotless lines and broad glass windows blend with the encompassing indigenous habitat, while the utilization of customary shoji screens and wooden subtleties gives proper respect to Kyoto's social legacy. This design combination makes a space that not just meets the useful prerequisites of a gathering community yet additionally draws in with the verifiable setting of its area.

Additionally, the Louver Pyramid in Paris, planned by designer I. M. Pei and finished in 1989, addresses an agreeable mix of innovation inside a verifiable setting. The pyramid, built of glass and steel, fills in as the primary access to the Louver Historical center, one of the world's biggest and most notorious social establishments. The juxtaposition of the pyramid's mathematical structure against the old style engineering of the Louver makes a striking visual difference, starting an exchange among old and contemporary plan. The Louver Pyramid remains as an image of the historical center's obligation to embracing the new while safeguarding its rich social heritage.

With regards to strict design, the Sheik Zayed Fantastic Mosque in Abu Dhabi represents the combination of custom and advancement. Finished in 2007, the mosque's plan draws motivation from different Islamic design styles while consolidating contemporary components. The utilization of white marble, perplexing mathematical examples, and customary calligraphy reflects Islamic creative practices, while the extensive size, present day materials, and best in class innovation exhibit a pledge to contemporary plan standards. The Sheik Zayed Excellent Mosque remains as a demonstration of the persevering through pertinence of conventional Islamic engineering in a quickly developing world.

Moving into the domain of inside plan, the combination of custom and advancement frequently unfurls in spaces that flawlessly coordinate authentic components with contemporary feel. The Aman Tokyo lodging, arranged in the Otemachi region, gives a convincing model. Housed in a cutting edge high rise, the lodging's insides honor conventional Japanese plan using regular materials, sliding shoji screens, and a quelled variety range. The juxtaposition of these customary components against the smooth innovation of the structure makes a quiet and thoughtful climate, offering visitors a remarkable encounter that spans the past and the present.

In the space of workmanship, specialists frequently draw in with the combination of custom and advancement to make works that reflect both verifiable impacts and contemporary sensibilities. Chinese craftsman Zhang Xiaogang's canvases, for example, investigate the crossing point of conventional Chinese representation and present day mental profundity. His series of "Bloodline" artworks, which started during the 1990s, draw motivation from traditional Chinese family pictures.

Notwithstanding, Zhang mixes these works with a cutting edge wind, utilizing strange and fanciful components to convey the mind boggling transaction of individual and aggregate character in a quickly evolving China.

Essentially, the contemporary craftsmanship scene in India mirrors a combination of customary creative procedures with present day articulations. Specialists like Bharti Kher mix antiquated Indian iconography, for example, the bindi, with contemporary topics, making works that overcome any issues among custom and advancement. Kher's specialty is a discourse between the social images well established from before and the difficulties and changes of the present.

In the realm of style, architects explore the fragile harmony among custom and advancement, drawing motivation from social legacy while pushing the limits of contemporary plan. The kimono, a conventional Japanese piece of clothing with a set of experiences traversing hundreds of years, has tracked down reverberation in current style. Fashioners like Yohji Yamamoto and Rei Kawakubo have integrated the kimono's outline and texture into their vanguard manifestations, mixing customary craftsmanship with a contemporary edge. This combination of conventional article of clothing development with present day plan sensibilities has added to the worldwide enthusiasm for Japanese style.

In like manner, in the domain of Indian style, fashioners, for example, Sabyasachi Mukherjee have acquired global praise for their capacity to mix conventional craftsmanship with current feel. Sabyasachi's manifestations frequently highlight complex hand-weaving, customary materials, and one of a kind enlivened outlines, making a particular style that resounds with both Indian and worldwide crowds. The creator's prosperity lies in his proficient combination of customary methods with a contemporary plan language.

The combination of custom and innovation isn't restricted to actual spaces or unmistakable curios; it reaches out into the computerized domain, where innovation turns into a material for social articulation. Computer games, as intelligent and vivid computerized encounters, give an interesting stage to investigating this combination. Games like "Phantom of Tsushima" draw motivation from verifiable Japanese scenes, engineering, and social practices while utilizing state of the art innovation to make an outwardly staggering and connecting with experience. The game's careful scrupulousness in reproducing conventional Japanese feel inside a cutting edge gaming structure exhibits the potential for innovation to overcome any issues between the old and the new.

In the domain of music, craftsmen frequently investigate the combination of conventional sounds with contemporary types, making a half breed sonic scene. The Indian old style music team, Pandit Ravi Shankar and Ustad Zakir Hussain, embody this combination through their joint efforts that mix the old practice of traditional ragas with present day instrumentation.

The sitar, a conventional Indian string instrument, tracks down reverberation with contemporary percussion and worldwide melodic impacts, bringing about an agreeable combination of the immortal and the contemporary.

The combination of custom and innovation isn't without its intricacies and difficulties. Finding some kind of harmony requires a nuanced comprehension of social legacy, a receptiveness to development, and an aversion to the advancing necessities and yearnings of social orders. Now and again, the combination might prompt the reevaluation of customs, testing traditional standards and offering new viewpoints on social personality. This should be visible in contemporary dance frames that draw from customary developments however consolidate present day strategies, making a combination that addresses the developing idea of imaginative articulation.

Urban areas, as unique centers of human action, frequently exemplify the combination of custom and advancement in their metropolitan scenes. Tokyo, for instance, features an extraordinary mix of old practices and state of the art innovation. The juxtaposition of Shinto hallowed places against the setting of neon-lit high rises mirrors the city's capacity to consistently incorporate its rich history with the requests of a cutting edge city. This combination isn't only shallow; it penetrates the lifestyle, from conventional tea functions to the most recent headways in mechanical technology and man-made consciousness.

In Istanbul, the Hagia Sophia gives an actual epitome of the city's layered history. Initially worked as a house of God in the sixth hundred years, changed over into a mosque during the Ottoman time, and later changed into a historical center in the twentieth 100 years, the Hagia Sophia mirrors the city's capacity to embrace and safeguard its different social legacy. The new choice to change over it back into a mosque highlights the continuous discussion among custom and innovation with regards to cultural and political elements.

The combination of custom and advancement likewise tracks down articulation in the culinary world, where conventional recipes and cooking procedures coincide with contemporary gastronomy. Prestigious cooks frequently draw motivation from neighborhood culinary customs while consolidating inventive ways to deal with make dishes that mirror a feeling of spot and time. The worldwide fame of combination cooking, which mixes flavors and methods from various culinary customs, embodies the continuous discourse between the old and the new in the domain of food.

All in all, the combination of custom and advancement is a complex and developing peculiarity that pervades each feature of human articulation. It's anything but a static harmony however a powerful exchange, a consistent discussion between the past and the present. This combination isn't tied in with deleting the past or dismissing custom; rather, it is a festival of the continuum of human imagination, flexibility, and versatility.

As social orders explore the intricacies of a quickly impacting world, the combination of custom and advancement fills in as a compass, directing the way toward a future where the wealth of social legacy joins with the conceivable outcomes of development.

3.4 Sustainability in Luxury Architecture

Maintainability in extravagance design addresses a change in perspective, a takeoff from traditional ideas of plushness that focus on excess to the detriment of ecological obligation. In a period set apart by developing familiarity with environmental change and the pressing requirement for reasonable practices, the convergence of extravagance and supportability challenges customary discernments and reclassifies creating esteemed and ecologically cognizant designs.

Extravagance engineering has for some time been related with self importance, sumptuous materials, and energy-escalated plans. Notwithstanding, as the worldwide cognizance shifts towards natural obligation, the extravagance area is adjusting to integrate reasonable practices without settling on the quintessence of lavishness. The fuse of green structure standards, sustainable power sources, and eco-accommodating materials into extravagance design mirrors a pledge to both stylish refinement and natural stewardship.

The One Focal Park improvement in Sydney, Australia, planned by engineer Jean Nouvel in a joint effort with botanist Patrick Blanc, fills in as an eminent illustration of extravagance design embracing supportability. Finished in 2013, the improvement highlights two private pinnacles enhanced with rich vertical nurseries. These nurseries not just upgrade the tasteful allure of the structures yet in addition add to biodiversity, further develop air quality, and give protection, decreasing the general energy utilization of the designs. One Focal Park embodies how maintainability can be consistently incorporated into extravagance engineering, making an agreeable harmony between human-made structures and the regular habitat.

The idea of supportability stretches out past individual structures to whole eco-accommodating networks. The idea of "ecoluxury" has arisen, underlining the formation of top of the line private spaces that focus on natural maintainability and social obligation. The Green Town in Bali, Indonesia, planned by draftsman Elora Strong and her group at Ibuku, embodies this idea. Involving complicatedly planned bamboo homes, the Green Town is a demonstration of the capability of maintainable materials and development procedures. Bamboo, a quickly developing and sustainable asset, shapes the essential structure material, and the plan standards focus on energy effectiveness and negligible natural effect. This extravagance local area grandstands that lavishness can coincide with a promise to biological obligation.

As extravagance design embraces maintainability, notorious designs all over the planet are going through eco-accommodating changes. The Domain State Working in New York City, an image of structural loftiness, went through a huge retrofitting in 2010 to improve its energy proficiency.

The redesign incorporated the establishment of energy-proficient windows, lighting updates, and a cutting edge building the board framework. The Domain Express Structure's obligation to manageability shows the way that even noteworthy milestones can embrace green practices without undermining their social and compositional importance.

In the domain of cordiality, extravagance resorts are progressively embracing maintainable practices to speak to naturally cognizant voyagers. The Soneva Fushi resort in the Maldives stands apart as a trailblazer in reasonable extravagance. The hotel's manors are built utilizing recovered wood, and energy is obtained from sun powered chargers. Squander the executives rehearses focus on reusing and treating the soil, limiting the retreat's biological impression. Soneva Fushi shows the way that extravagance friendliness can be inseparable from ecological stewardship, giving visitors lavish encounters while keeping a guarantee to supportability.

The idea of feasible extravagance isn't restricted to private and accommodation areas; it stretches out to business spaces too. The Edge, a place of business in Amsterdam, grandstands how corporate engineering can be both extravagant and reasonable. Planned by PLP Engineering and created by PLP Engineering and D/DOCK, The Edge integrates imaginative highlights, for example, savvy lighting frameworks, water reaping, and a roof garden with colonies of bees. The structure's energy effectiveness and green drives deserve it the title of the world's most reasonable place of business. The Edge reclassifies the conventional office space, demonstrating that manageability can be consistently incorporated into the professional workplace without settling for less on solace or style.

The reception of manageable extravagance standards in design isn't exclusively a reaction to ecological worries; it is likewise an essential reaction to changing customer inclinations. The advanced extravagance purchaser is progressively earth cognizant, looking for items and encounters that line up with their qualities. This change in buyer conduct has provoked extravagance brands and engineers to focus on supportability as a critical part of their contributions. The reconciliation of green highlights, energy-proficient innovations, and eco-accommodating materials enjoys become a serious benefit for extravagance properties.

Engineers and planners are answering the interest for manageable extravagance by pushing the limits of advancement. The Bosco Verticale (Vertical Backwoods) in Milan, planned by Stefano Boeri Architetti, represents an earth shattering way to deal with feasible extravagance living. Finished in 2014, this private complex highlights two pinnacles covered with a lavish timberland of trees and plants. The upward backwoods not just improves the stylish allure of the structures yet in addition adds to air decontamination and biodiversity. The Bosco Verticale sets another norm for practical extravagance engineering, demonstrating that very good quality private living can coincide agreeably with nature.

In the domain of social establishments, galleries are likewise embracing maintainable practices in their building plans. The California Foundation of Sciences in San Francisco, planned by modeler Renzo Piano, is an eminent model. Finished in 2008, the historical center elements a living rooftop with local plants that give protection and retain water. Normal ventilation and daylighting procedures diminish the requirement for counterfeit lighting and cooling. The California Foundation of Sciences represents how social establishments can show others how its done, showing the way that manageability can be a fundamental piece of compositional greatness.

The idea of maintainable extravagance reaches out to the style business, where creators are progressively consolidating eco-accommodating practices into their lead stores. Stella McCartney, a trailblazer in reasonable style, has made an interpretation of her obligation to ecological obligation into the plan of her stores. The Stella McCartney lead store in London highlights recovered wood, energy-productive lighting, and other eco-accommodating components, lining up with the brand's ethos of savagery free and manageable style. This approach mirrors a more extensive pattern in the extravagance retail area, where manageability is turning into a vital thought in store plan and tasks.

In the domain of metropolitan preparation, the idea of manageable extravagance is impacting the improvement of whole eco-accommodating areas. The Bo01 locale in Malmö, Sweden, is a perfect representation of metropolitan arranging that focuses on supportability and extravagance. Finished in 2001, Bo01 consolidates energy-effective structures, green spaces, and eco-accommodating transportation choices. The locale's obligation to supportability has changed it into an attractive and upscale neighborhood, exhibiting that extravagance can be inseparable from earth cognizant metropolitan living.

Developments in materials assume a pivotal part chasing manageable extravagance design. The utilization of reused and reused materials, as well as the investigation of elective development techniques, add to diminishing the natural effect of extravagance structures. The Zeitz Gallery of Contemporary Craftsmanship Africa (MOCAA) in Cape Town, South Africa, reused a noteworthy grain storehouse into a state of the art social establishment. The structure's inventive utilization of substantial cylinders, known as "padded glass," makes an exceptional and energy-proficient exterior. This versatile reuse project not just jam a piece of the city's modern legacy yet additionally exhibits the capability of supportable extravagance in the domain of social design.

The coordination of environmentally friendly power sources is a sign of economical extravagance design. Sunlight based chargers, wind turbines, and other efficient power energy innovations are becoming indispensable parts of top of the line private and business improvements. The Pearl Stream Pinnacle in Guangzhou, China, planned by Skidmore, Owings and Merrill, is a high rise that represents this methodology.

Finished in 2013, the pinnacle highlights coordinated breeze turbines, sun powered chargers, and a high level twofold skin drape wall framework that upgrades energy productivity. The Pearl Waterway Pinnacle's obligation to environmentally friendly power sources grandstands that supportability can be flawlessly incorporated into the plan of famous high rises.

The quest for reasonable extravagance isn't without its difficulties. Adjusting the requests of lavishness with the imperatives of eco-accommodating practices requires a sensitive dance of imagination, development, and faithful navigation. The expense of maintainable advances and materials, albeit progressively diminishing, can in any case present monetary difficulties for extravagance designers. Also, accomplishing agreement on manageability norms and certificates inside the extravagance area is a continuous interaction, as various locales and enterprises might have differed ways to deal with characterizing and estimating natural execution.

Chapter 4

Culinary Mastery

Culinary dominance, a combination of workmanship and science, addresses the zenith of gastronomic accomplishment. It rises above the simple demonstration of cooking, developing into a complex dance of flavors, surfaces, and introductions that dazzle the faculties. As a culinary craftsman explores the domain of fixings, procedures, and social impacts, they leave on an excursion that investigates the rich embroidery of culinary practices while pushing the limits of development. This investigation of culinary authority traverses assorted cooking styles, from the encouraging hug of conventional dishes to the vanguard manifestations that rethink the actual embodiment of feasting.

At its center, culinary dominance is about a significant comprehension of fixings — their flavors, surfaces, and subtleties. The craft of choosing and obtaining the best fixings is the establishment whereupon culinary greatness is assembled. From the energy of privately obtained produce to the intricacy of intriguing flavors and the deliciousness of impeccably matured meats, cooks wind around together an orchestra of flavors that reflect both the terroir of their environmental factors and the worldwide impacts that shape contemporary food.

In customary culinary societies, for example, French food, the accentuation on fixing quality is principal. The idea of "terroir," which typifies the one of a kind qualities of a district's dirt, environment, and topography, highlights the significance of neighborhood fixings in making dishes that reverberate with a feeling of spot. French culinary experts, as Auguste Escoffier and Paul Bocuse, have made a permanent imprint on the culinary world by raising the significance of new, occasional, and privately obtained fixings.

In the domain of Asian cooking styles, dominance stretches out to the craft of adjusting flavors and surfaces, frequently directed by standards like yin and yang in Chinese culinary way of thinking or the five essential preferences for Japanese food. Japanese cooks, especially in the domain of sushi, grandstand an unmatched accuracy in blade abilities and an unflinching obligation to the freshest fish. The sensitive interchange of umami, pleasantness, sharpness, harshness, and pungency is painstakingly coordinated to make an amicable culinary encounter.

Past the authority of individual fixings, culinary greatness is appeared in the methods utilized in the kitchen. From old style French culinary procedures, for example, sous vide and sautéing, to the complex imaginativeness of Japanese kaiseki, each culinary practice has own collection of strategies request accuracy, ability, and an instinctive comprehension of the groundbreaking idea of intensity and time.

In the realm of cake and baking, gourmet specialists like Pierre Hermé and Dominique Ansel epitomize the levels of culinary authority. The fragile specialty of making impeccably covered croissants, creating mind boggling sugar forms, or accomplishing the ideal ascent and piece structure in a soufflé requires both specialized ability and a sharp imaginative reasonableness. Baked good culinary specialists, frequently alluded to as "pâtissiers," participate in a fragile dance among accuracy and imagination to create treats that are outwardly dazzling as well as an orchestra of flavors.

The approach of atomic gastronomy, promoted by gourmet specialists like Ferran Adrià of elBulli, further extended the conceivable outcomes of culinary advancement. By taking apart and recreating natural fixings, sub-atomic gastronomy tested conventional thoughts of surface and show. Procedures like spherification, frothing, and freeze-drying became devices in the culinary weapons store, permitting cooks to make dishes that made heads spin and offered cafes a multisensory experience.

Culinary authority is additionally profoundly entwined with social legacy and narrating. In each dish, there lies a story — a story of customs went down through ages, an impression of verifiable impacts, and a statement of character. This is clear in the unpredictable flavor mixes of Indian food, where the mix of fragrant flavors recounts an account of shipping lanes and social trades. Likewise, the rich embroidery of flavors in Mexican food mirrors a combination of native fixings with Spanish and other European impacts.

The idea of the "gourmet expert as a craftsman" has acquired unmistakable quality as of late, with culinary bosses pushing the limits of imagination and self-articulation. The kitchen turns into a material, and each plate a masterpiece that mirrors the gourmet expert's extraordinary point of view and culinary way of thinking. Prestigious gourmet specialists like Massimo Bottura of Osteria Francescana and Heston Blumenthal of The Fat Duck have embraced vanguard draws near, using whimsical fixings and strategies to challenge assumptions of taste and show.

Culinary authority isn't bound to the domain of haute cooking; it penetrates each edge of the culinary scene, from road food merchants to neighborhood bistros. The dominance lies in the capacity to change humble fixings into phenomenal encounters, rising above the limits of financial plan or setting. Road food merchants in urban communities like Bangkok or Mexico City exhibit a natural comprehension of flavors and surfaces, making dishes that are delectable as well as well established in neighborhood culinary customs.

The feasting experience, as well, is an essential piece of culinary dominance. Past the flavors on the plate, the mood, administration, and scrupulousness add to making a noteworthy culinary excursion. Eateries like El Celler de Could Roca in Spain and Noma in Denmark at any point have reclassified the feasting experience, with careful regard for each part of the dinner.

The collaboration between the front of house and the kitchen, the cautiously organized wine pairings, and the narrating behind each dish raise the eating experience to an artistic expression.

The manageability development has additionally made a permanent imprint on culinary dominance. Gourmet specialists all over the planet are progressively aware of the natural effect of their specialty, prompting a re-examination of obtaining rehearses, squander decrease, and an emphasis on nearby and occasional fixings. The ranch to-table development, supported by cooks like Dan Hairdresser of Blue Slope at Stone Horse shelters, stresses the significance of an immediate association among makers and purchasers, encouraging a more economical and straightforward food framework.

The combination of innovation and culinary dominance has led to imaginative methodologies in the kitchen. From accuracy cooking with sous vide machines to the utilization of 3D printing for making complex palatable plans, culinary specialists are embracing innovation to improve their inventive abilities. Computer generated reality and expanded the truth are additionally finding applications in the culinary world, offering vivid eating encounters that connect every one of the faculties.

The idea of culinary the travel industry has acquired prevalence, with voyagers looking for fascinating objections as well as interesting food encounters. Urban areas like Tokyo, Barcelona, and Bangkok have become culinary capitals, drawing guests from around the world anxious to relish the neighborhood fortes and experience the authority of prestigious gourmet specialists. Culinary visits, cooking classes, and food celebrations have become essential pieces of movement agendas, exhibiting the worldwide interest with the specialty of gastronomy.

The job of culinary specialists has developed past the bounds of the kitchen. Culinary bosses are presently powerful figures, molding food patterns, supporting for manageability, and utilizing their foundation to resolve social issues. Cook driven drives, for example, Massimo Bottura's Nourishment for Soul, plan to battle food squander and advance social inclusivity through local area kitchens. Culinary instruction projects and mentorship drives further add to the advancement of the up and coming age of cooks, guaranteeing the coherence of culinary dominance.

The effect of culinary dominance stretches out to media and mainstream society, with a wealth of cooking shows, narratives, and web-based entertainment stages devoted to the craft of food. VIP gourmet experts, like Gordon Ramsay and Anthony Bourdain, have become easily recognized names, bringing the universe of gastronomy into the standard. Stages like Instagram and YouTube have democratized food photography and culinary narrating, permitting cooks and food lovers the same to impart their manifestations to a worldwide crowd.

4.1 Gastronomic Delights

Gastronomic pleasures, an ensemble of flavors and surfaces, address the zenith of culinary imaginativeness. It is an excursion through different culinary customs, where cooks, both customary and vanguard, change crude fixings into show-stoppers that entice the taste buds and summon a tactile encounter dissimilar to some other. The universe of gastronomy is a festival of imagination, culture, and craftsmanship, where each dish recounts a story and each chomp is a disclosure.

At the core of gastronomic pleasures is the investigation of fixings. From the clamoring markets of Marrakech to the immaculate fish markets of Tokyo, culinary experts set out on a journey for the best and freshest produce, meats, and flavors. The craft of fixing determination is a demonstration of a gourmet expert's insightful sense of taste and a comprehension of the basic structure blocks of flavor. The excursion starts with the crude material of nature, and the cook, similar to a craftsman, shapes it into a culinary work of art.

Culinary practices all over the planet exhibit the wealth of neighborhood fixings and the social accounts woven into each dish. In Italy, the straightforwardness of an impeccably created pasta dish, for example, spaghetti aglio e olio, depends on the nature of olive oil, garlic, and a sprinkle of red pepper drops. The embodiment of Japanese cooking is caught in the craft of sushi, where the kind of each carefully cut fish mirrors the flawless waters from which it is obtained. In Mexico, the lively tints of a mole poblano recount an account of old civilizations, with fixings like chocolate, chilies, and flavors consolidating to make a perplexing and agreeable flavor profile.

The authority of cooking procedures is one more foundation of gastronomic enjoyments. From the accuracy of French culinary strategies to the strong and red hot techniques for Indian cooking, gourmet specialists improve their abilities to organize an ensemble of flavors. The singing intensity of a wok in a clamoring Chinese kitchen, the sluggish stewing of a French sauce, or the many-sided layering of flavors in a Moroccan tagine — this large number of procedures add to the nuanced and changed universe of gastronomy.

The universe of gastronomy isn't restricted to very good quality cafés and Michelin-featured foundations. Road food sellers in Bangkok, food slows down in Marrakech, and taco trucks in Los Angeles all assume a urgent part in the worldwide embroidery of culinary pleasures. These unassuming settings frequently produce the absolute most noteworthy and genuine gastronomic encounters, where effortlessness and expertise combine to make dishes that reverberate with local people and guests the same.

The craft of gastronomy isn't just about fulfilling hunger; about making an encounter connects every one of the faculties. The visual show of a dish, the smell that floats through the air, the sizzle and pop in the kitchen — all add to the vivid idea of gastronomic joys.

Eminent culinary specialists, like Ferran Adrià of elBulli, have taken this tactile experience higher than ever, utilizing sub-atomic gastronomy to play with surfaces, temperatures, and introductions in manners that challenge customary thoughts of food.

Lately, the idea of ranch to-table eating has acquired unmistakable quality, mirroring a more profound association among makers and shoppers. Eateries and cooks focused on this way of thinking focus on neighborhood and occasional fixings, praising the abundance of adjacent ranches and makers. This approach not just improves the newness and nature of the fixings yet in addition cultivates a more practical and naturally cognizant food framework.

Gastronomic joys likewise reach out past the plate to the domain of drinks. The universe of wine, with its rich terroirs and varietals, supplements and improves the eating experience. Sommeliers, with their mastery in matching wines with dishes, assume an essential part in hoisting the generally gastronomic experience. Create mixed drinks, distinctive brews, and specialty teas further add to the assorted scene of refreshments that go with and improve the joy of feasting.

The social meaning of gastronomy couldn't possibly be more significant. Culinary customs are naturally connected to a locale's set of experiences, geology, and social texture. In India, the variety of local foods mirrors the country's rich woven artwork of dialects, religions, and customs. In the American South, dishes like gumbo and grill recount an account of social combination, molded by the union of African, European, and Local American impacts. The demonstration of sharing a dinner is an all inclusive human experience, encouraging associations and making a common feeling of personality.

Gastronomic the travel industry has turned into a huge worldwide pattern, with voyagers looking for pleasant scenes as well as important food encounters. Culinary objections, from the wine districts of Bordeaux to the road food markets of Bangkok, attract guests anxious to submerge themselves the neighborhood gastronomic scene. Food and travel become interlaced as individuals investigate new societies through their culinary practices, making a worldwide exchange where flavors, strategies, and stories are shared.

The development of gastronomic enjoyments is likewise obvious in the developing pattern of spring up eateries, food celebrations, and co-operative feasting encounters. Eminent gourmet experts frequently team up with their friends from various culinary customs, making combination dishes that exhibit the cross-fertilization of flavors and procedures. Spring up cafés, with their fleeting nature, offer gourmet experts a material for trial and error and coffee shops a chance to encounter something interesting and unforeseen.

In the period of web-based entertainment, the introduction of gastronomic enjoyments has taken on new aspects. Stages like Instagram and YouTube have changed the manner in which individuals draw in with food, transforming culinary experts into powerhouses and burger joints into pundits.

The visual charm of an impeccably plated dish, caught in a photo, can bring out an instinctive reaction and add to the ubiquity and progress of an eatery. Notwithstanding, this visual-driven approach likewise brings up issues about the effect of web-based entertainment on the validness of the feasting experience.

Culinary training and mentorship assume an imperative part in forming the eventual fate of gastronomy. Culinary schools and apprenticeships furnish hopeful gourmet specialists with the abilities and information expected to explore the complicated universe of expert kitchens. Mentorship from prepared gourmet experts, with their abundance of involvement and bits of knowledge, is priceless in encouraging the up and coming age of culinary bosses. Programs like the Bocuse d'Or, a renowned global culinary contest, feature the ability and development rising up out of culinary schooling.

The job of gastronomy in tending to worldwide difficulties is progressively perceived. Food manageability, moral obtaining, and diminishing food squander have become focal subjects in the culinary world. Cooks, like René Redzepi of Noma, have embraced a zero-squander theory, imaginatively utilizing neglected or disposed of fixings to make lovely dishes. The idea of "nose-to-tail" and "root-to-stem" cooking epitomize a pledge to limiting food squander and expanding the utility of each and every fixing.

The combination of innovation and gastronomy has prompted creative methodologies in the kitchen. High level kitchen apparatuses, accuracy cooking methods, and information driven culinary trial and error have become necessary pieces of the cutting edge kitchen. The utilization of advanced mechanics in food planning, 3D printing for eatable manifestations, and computer generated reality for vivid feasting encounters are pushing the limits of what is conceivable in the domain of gastronomy.

The idea of gastronomic joys is profoundly interlaced with the possibility of extravagance and festivity. From the intricate blowouts of old civic establishments to the cutting edge festivity meals, food has forever been a focal point of upbeat events. The demonstration of sharing a feast is a custom that rises above social limits, uniting individuals in snapshots of festivity, reflection, and association.

Gastronomic the travel industry has turned into a huge worldwide pattern, with explorers looking for pleasant scenes as well as paramount food encounters. Culinary objections, from the wine districts of Bordeaux to the road food markets of Bangkok, attract guests anxious to drench themselves the neighborhood gastronomic scene.

4.2 Michelin-Starred Dining

Michelin-featured eating, an encapsulation of culinary greatness, addresses a culinary excursion where imaginativeness, development, and careful craftsmanship unite on the plate. The Michelin Guide, laid out quite a long time back by the tire organization Michelin, has turned into the most lofty and sought-after honor in the culinary world. Granting stars to cafés in light of the mastery of mysterious controllers, the aide has changed eating into an encounter that goes past simple food, lifting it to a type of high craftsmanship.

At the core of Michelin-featured eating is the quest for flawlessness. A pursuit starts with the determination of excellent fixings, obtained with a resolute obligation to quality and newness. Eminent cooks, going for the gold Michelin stars, lay out associations with nearby ranchers, anglers, and craftsmans to get the best produce. The provenance of fixings turns into an account, every part recounting an account of the land, the ocean, and the fastidious consideration taken to carry it to the plate.

The standards for granting Michelin stars are tough and envelop a bunch of elements, including the nature of fixings, the expertise in readiness, the blend of flavors, the imagination in show, and the general eating experience. Procuring a Michelin star isn't simply an affirmation of a gourmet expert's culinary ability; it is an acknowledgment of an eatery's obligation to greatness across each part of the feasting venture.

The idea of Michelin stars was at first presented by the Michelin Guide as a method for advancing travel and, thus, the utilization of vehicles and tires. Throughout the long term, the Michelin stars have developed into the most esteemed and powerful culinary honors all around the world. A three-star rating is the zenith, meaning extraordinary food, worth a unique excursion; two stars address phenomenal cooking, worth a diversion; and one star indicates a generally excellent eatery, worth halting for. The Michelin stars have turned into an image of culinary renown, impacting the standing and outcome of cafés all over the planet.

The feasting experience at Michelin-featured cafés rises above the demonstration of eating; it is a multisensory venture that connects with sight, smell, taste, and contact. The careful scrupulousness is obvious from the second benefactors enter the café — the feeling, the table settings, the lighting — all aligned to make an environment that supplements the culinary imaginativeness going to unfurl. The quieted tones of a top notch food room, the sparkle of cleaned flatware, and the mindful help add to a general mood of complexity and extravagance.

The craft of plating, a sign of Michelin-featured eating, changes each dish into a visual magnum opus. Gourmet specialists carefully organize parts on the plate, taking into account tone, surface, and adjust to make an outwardly staggering show. Each component fills a need, adding to the general congruity of the dish.

The visual allure of Michelin-featured dishes is frequently all around as significant as the taste, and gourmet experts endeavor to inspire a profound reaction from coffee shops with the sheer magnificence of their manifestations.

Flavor, obviously, stays vital in Michelin-featured eating. The combination of fixings, the layering of tastes, and the intricacy of flavor profiles feature the cook's dominance of the culinary expressions. Each nibble is a disclosure, an excursion through an orchestra of tastes that develop on the sense of taste. The quest for the ideal equilibrium of flavors, the exchange of sweet and exquisite, the differentiation of surfaces — these are the signs of Michelin-featured cooking.

The tasting menu, a typical element in Michelin-featured foundations, permits gourmet experts to grandstand their imagination and deal cafes an organized excursion through their culinary vision. Tasting menus frequently include a movement of dishes, each structure on the past one, making a story that unfurls with each course. The experience is likened to a gastronomic story, where the culinary specialist turns into a narrator, directing burger joints through a painstakingly created account of flavors and surfaces.

The universe of Michelin-featured eating isn't restricted to a particular cooking. A worldwide peculiarity embraces a different scope of culinary practices. French haute cooking, with its accentuation on method and refinement, has for quite some time been related with Michelin stars. Alain Ducasse, Paul Bocuse, and Joël Robuchon are among the amazing French gourmet specialists whose foundations have procured various Michelin stars, setting the norm for culinary greatness.

Italian food, with its accentuation on effortlessness and the nature of fixings, has likewise found a spot among Michelin-featured cafés. Massimo Bottura's Osteria Francescana, situated in Modena, Italy, is eminent for its creative way to deal with conventional Italian dishes, procuring it three Michelin stars and worldwide approval. The culinary scene of Spain, especially Catalonia, flaunts various Michelin-featured eateries, with El Celler de Can Roca in Girona reliably positioning among the world's ideal.

The ascent of Asian food on the worldwide culinary stage is reflected in the Michelin Guide's acknowledgment of remarkable cafés in the locale. Japan, with its commitment to accuracy and regard for occasional fixings, has a powerful Michelin-featured scene. Tokyo, specifically, has more Michelin-featured cafés than some other city, with Sukiyabashi Jiro, a minuscule sushi foundation, holding three stars. Across Asia, from Hong Kong to Bangkok, culinary specialists are mixing conventional methods with present day development to procure desired Michelin stars.

In the US, Michelin stars are a characteristic of differentiation for cafés in urban communities like New York, San Francisco, and Chicago. The French Clothing in California's Napa Valley, drove by Cook Thomas Keller, is inseparable from culinary greatness and has been granted three Michelin stars. The gastronomic scene in Chicago, with eateries like Alinea and Elegance, has earned worldwide respect, adding to the city's standing as a culinary objective.

The excursion towards Michelin fame is requesting and requires relentless devotion from gourmet specialists and their groups. The quest for flawlessness frequently involves extended periods, careful meticulousness, and a steady drive for development. Gourmet experts should explore the fragile harmony among custom and inventiveness, drawing on their culinary legacy while pushing the limits of what is conceivable. The strain to keep up with Michelin stars, once acquired, is similarly extraordinary, as culinary experts endeavor to reliably convey remarkable eating encounters.

The effect of Michelin stars on a café's prosperity couldn't possibly be more significant. A solitary star can launch an eatery into the worldwide spotlight, drawing in knowing coffee shops and culinary fans from around the world. A few stars lift an eatery to the echelon of culinary significance, setting its place among the best foundations. The acknowledgment from the Michelin Guide isn't simply a respectable symbol; it is an approval of a culinary expert's deep rooted commitment to the art.

Regardless of the esteem related with Michelin stars, the framework has confronted its portion of reactions. Some contend that the rules for granting stars can be misty, prompting hypothesis and discussion inside the culinary local area. The secrecy of Michelin examiners, while planned to keep up with unprejudiced nature, has likewise been a wellspring of secret and interest. Furthermore, the accentuation on a particular top notch food model has been tested by the people who advocate for a more extensive meaning of culinary greatness that incorporates different culinary practices and more easygoing eating encounters.

The monetary ramifications of Michelin stars are significant. The convergence of benefactors looking for the Michelin-featured experience adds to the monetary outcome of cafés and the encompassing neighborliness industry. Urban communities with a high convergence of Michelin-featured foundations frequently experience a lift in the travel industry, with food devotees leaving on culinary journeys to enjoy the manifestations of eminent gourmet specialists. The financial effect stretches out to neighborhood providers, ranchers, and craftsmans who benefit from the expanded interest for excellent fixings.

Lately, the idea of manageability has acquired conspicuousness in the culinary world, including among Michelin-featured cafés. Gourmet specialists and foundations are progressively centered around moral obtaining, squander decrease, and earth cognizant practices.

The crossing point of Michelin-featured eating and supportability is obvious in drives like zero-squander kitchens, privately obtained menus, and a promise to limiting the carbon impression of the feasting experience.

The democratization of gastronomy, worked with by virtual entertainment and the ascent of culinary powerhouses, has extended the scope of Michelin-featured feasting. Cafes can now investigate and value the culinary manifestations of prestigious gourmet specialists without genuinely visiting their cafés. Virtual encounters, cooking shows, and online substance give looks into the universe of Michelin-featured kitchens, making the specialty of high end food more open to a worldwide crowd.

4.3 Celebrity Chefs and Signature Menus

Big name gourmet experts, a peculiarity that has ascended to noticeable quality in late many years, have become culinary symbols whose impact stretches out a long ways past the limits of the kitchen. These culinary maestros, known for their mystique, development, and unmistakable styles, have accomplished big name status through a blend of ability, media presence, and enterprising sharpness. Key to their allure is the making of mark menus — culinary creations that embody their one of a kind culinary ways of thinking and grandstand their capacity to push the limits of taste and show.

The development of big name gourmet experts can be followed back to the late twentieth century when the culinary world went through a change, impelled by the coming of TV, the ascent of food media, and a rising interest with gastronomy. Gourmet experts progressed from in the background kitchen figures to charming characters who enraptured crowds with their culinary ability. Trailblazers like Julia Kid, with her notable Program "The French Culinary expert," established the groundwork for the VIP gourmet specialist peculiarity, showing the way that cooking could be engaging and open.

In the contemporary culinary scene, big name gourmet experts have become social powerhouses with worldwide reach. Any semblance of Gordon Ramsay, Jamie Oliver, Anthony Bourdain, and Nigella Lawson play rose above the customary parts of culinary experts, growing their presence into TV, distributing, and item supports. Their prevalence isn't exclusively founded on culinary expertise yet in addition on the capacity to associate with crowds, recount convincing stories, and explore the media scene.

One characterizing part of a superstar cook's image is the formation of mark menus. These menus are not only an assortment of dishes; they are culinary declarations that mirror the gourmet specialist's character, impacts, and imaginative vision. Each dish is cautiously organized to feature the gourmet expert's dominance of fixings, strategies, and flavors. The mark menu turns into a culinary excursion for burger joints, an investigation of the cook's culinary world embodied in a painstakingly created grouping of courses.

Gordon Ramsay, an imposing presence in both the culinary and TV circles, is famous for his unique menus that ooze class, striking flavors, and fastidious execution. Ramsay's multi-Michelin-featured eateries, for example, Gordon Ramsay at Regal Emergency clinic Street in London, include tasting menus that feature his ability in both traditional and current culinary strategies. Dishes like Hamburger Wellington, a Ramsay signature, grandstand his capacity to raise customary English charge to the levels of gastronomic greatness.

Jamie Oliver, known for his promotion of straightforward, healthy cooking, carries a particular ethos to his unique menus. Oliver's dishes are described by new, occasional fixings, lively tones, and an emphasis on openness. His eatery, Fifteen, which began as a social venture preparing impeded youth in the culinary expressions, highlights menus that underscore the delight of sharing food and the significance of local area.

Anthony Bourdain, a charming figure known for his investigation of worldwide foods and culinary narrating, made a permanent imprint on the culinary world before his less than ideal passing. Bourdain's particular menus, as found in his acclaimed café Brasserie Les Halles in New York City, mirrored his diverse preferences and appreciation for both top of the line and road level gastronomy. Bourdain's impact reached out past the kitchen, motivating an age of food fans to embrace culinary variety and experience.

Nigella Lawson, celebrated for her warm and agreeable style, has made signature menus that exemplify her adoration for solace food and extravagance. Lawson's recipes frequently highlight extravagant fixings, liberal treats, and a festival of the delights of home cooking. Her unique menu mirrors a culinary way of thinking that puts accentuation on the delight and sexiness of food, making her a symbol in the domain of home cooking.

The formation of a mark menu includes a careful cycle that goes past the simple blend of fixings. Big name culinary experts draw on a heap of impacts, from social practices to individual encounters, to shape the story of their menus. The menu turns into a material for self-articulation, permitting gourmet experts to impart their culinary character and reasoning to cafes.

Imaginative methods and culinary patterns likewise assume a significant part in molding mark menus. VIP gourmet specialists are frequently at the front of culinary development, embracing new cooking techniques, fixings, and introductions. Sub-atomic gastronomy, sous vide cooking, and the utilization of cutting edge methods have found a spot in the collection of gourmet experts like Heston Blumenthal, whose signature menus at The Fat Duck in Whinny, UK, are a demonstration of his limit pushing way to deal with gastronomy.

The idea of homestead to-table, with an accentuation on neighborhood and occasional fixings, has turned into a foundation of numerous big name culinary experts' unique menus.

Culinary specialists like Alice Waters, a trailblazer of the homestead to-table development, have supported the significance of practical, privately obtained produce. Waters' notable eatery Chez Panisse in Berkeley, California, exhibits a promise to the effortlessness of flavors and the honesty of fixings in her particular menus.

The improvement of a mark menu is certainly not a static cycle; it develops with the gourmet specialist's culinary excursion and the changing scene of gastronomy. Gourmet specialists might present new dishes, rethink works of art, and trial with novel ideas to keep their menus new and intelligent of their advancing viewpoints. The mark menu turns into a no nonsense element that reflects the gourmet specialist's development, impacts, and progressing investigation of the culinary expressions.

VIP cooks influence their image and impact to expand the scope of their unmistakable menus past the limits of their cafés. Cookbooks, TV programs, and computerized stages give a medium to gourmet experts to share their recipes, strategies, and culinary ways of thinking with a worldwide crowd. The distribution of a cookbook frequently turns into an expansion of the mark menu, permitting home cooks to reproduce the gourmet expert's dishes and experience a sample of their culinary world.

The peculiarity of spring up eateries and culinary occasions has additionally given big name cooks amazing open doors to exhibit their unique menus to assorted crowds. Pop-ups, whether transitory establishments or worldwide culinary visits, permit gourmet specialists to explore different avenues regarding new ideas, team up with peers, and draw in with fans in exceptional settings. These occasions frequently highlight selective dishes or varieties of mark things, making a feeling of energy and expectation among cafes.

Web-based entertainment, with its visual-driven nature, has turned into an amazing asset for big name gourmet experts to feature their particular menus and draw in with devotees. Stages like Instagram, Facebook, and Twitter permit culinary experts to share in the background looks at kitchen life, feature highlighted dishes, and associate with a worldwide local area of food lovers. The promptness of online entertainment empowers gourmet specialists to discuss straightforwardly with their crowd, cultivating a feeling of closeness and openness.

The effect of a superstar gourmet expert's unmistakable menu stretches out past the culinary domain; it adds to the general brand character and progress of the cook's ventures. The acknowledgment and prominence gathered through signature dishes can drive reservations, draw in media inclusion, and raise the gourmet expert's remaining in the cutthroat universe of gastronomy. Signature menus become a critical component in forming the story of a gourmet specialist's profession, assisting with characterizing their heritage and impact.

The globalization of culinary culture, worked with by movement and computerized availability, has intensified the impact of superstar gourmet experts and their particular menus. Eateries helmed by prestigious gourmet specialists have become objections in themselves, drawing food lovers from around the world. The capacity to encounter a big name gourmet specialist's unmistakable menu, whether at their lead eatery or a spring up occasion, has turned into a sought-after culinary journey for knowing burger joints.

Notwithstanding the fabulousness and achievement related with superstar cooks, challenges exist in keeping up with the respectability of their unmistakable menus across assorted areas and culinary scenes. Development of eatery realms, diversifying, and associations can introduce strategic and imaginative difficulties for cooks planning to repeat the pith of their particular menus in various settings. Adjusting the interest for consistency with the longing for development requires a fragile harmony.

The idea of big name culinary experts and mark menus has not been without analysis. Some contend that the religion of superstar can eclipse the culinary value of a cook's work, prompting an emphasis on character instead of substance. The commercialization of the superstar gourmet expert brand, with supports, product offerings, and media adventures, has provoked conversations about the realness of the culinary experience and the effect on the conventional job of cooks.

4.4 Culinary Innovation in Luxury Hospitality

Culinary development in extravagance neighborliness addresses an enamoring combination of imagination, expertise, and a guarantee to conveying unrivaled feasting encounters. The universe of extravagance eating is portrayed by a quest for greatness that goes past customary limits, pushing the envelope of culinary masterfulness. From cutting edge methods to the careful determination of intriguing and dazzling fixings, extravagance neighborliness foundations set new norms for gastronomic guilty pleasure, offering visitors an excursion into the unprecedented.

At the core of culinary development in extravagance friendliness lies a devotion to reclassifying the limits of taste, show, and generally eating experience. Prestigious gourmet experts and culinary groups in lavish lodgings and resorts are not happy with just fulfilling hunger; they plan to lift feasting to the level of a tactile display, where each component — flavor, smell, surface, and visual show — fits to make an extraordinary second.

The excursion into culinary development frequently starts with a profound investigation of fixings. Extravagance foundations source the best, freshest, and most selective produce, frequently laying out direct associations with nearby ranchers, foragers, and distinctive providers. The quest for novel and intriguing fixings turns into a sign of extravagance eating, where dishes are made with an emphasis on provenance, maintainability, and a festival of the terroir.

Cutting edge culinary procedures assume a crucial part in the development found in extravagance cordiality. Gourmet specialists in these foundations frequently draw motivation from the universe of atomic gastronomy, accuracy cooking strategies, and state of the art culinary advances. Procedures, for example, sous vide, spherification, and frothing are utilized to dismantle and reproduce recognizable fixings, making dishes that challenge regular thoughts and connect with coffee shops in a multisensory investigation.

The idea of the tasting menu, a cautiously organized grouping of dishes, turns into a material for culinary development in extravagance cordiality. These menus are not simply feasts; they are stories that unfurl with each course, directing burger joints through a gastronomic excursion. The tasting menu permits gourmet experts to grandstand their imagination, try different things with flavors and surfaces, and present a durable story that mirrors their culinary way of thinking.

Extravagance cordiality foundations frequently put vigorously in innovative work, encouraging a culture of trial and error and constant improvement. The kitchen turns into a research center where gourmet experts, alongside gifted culinary groups, push the limits of what is conceivable. The mission for advancement stretches out to the making of altogether new dishes, novel flavor mixes, and the improvement of mark procedures that put the foundation aside.

Show in extravagance neighborliness is raised to a work of art. Culinary specialists draw motivation from different sources, including workmanship, nature, and social impacts, to make outwardly staggering dishes that enthrall the faculties. The plate turns into a material, and each dish a show-stopper, with careful consideration given to variety, organization, and the general tasteful allure. The visual scene is a necessary piece of the extravagance eating experience, improving the general feeling of guilty pleasure and refinement.

The idea of experiential feasting becomes the dominant focal point in extravagance neighborliness. Past the bounds of the conventional eatery setting, extravagance foundations plan to make vivid culinary encounters that connect every one of the faculties. This might include gourmet specialist's tables with direct association with the culinary group, confidential eating encounters in remarkable settings, or even culinary occasions and celebrations that grandstand the zenith of gastronomic development.

The coordination of innovation into the culinary experience is an eminent pattern in extravagance neighborliness. From intuitive menus on tablets to increased reality-improved eating encounters, innovation is outfit to make a feeling of curiosity and commitment. Augmented reality might be utilized to move cafes to various culinary scenes, improving the narrating part of the eating experience.

Coordinated efforts with prestigious gourmet specialists and specialists from different fields have turned into a sign of culinary development in extravagance cordiality.

Foundations frequently welcome superstar culinary experts, sommeliers, or even craftsmen to team up on unique menus or occasions. These joint efforts bring different viewpoints, mastery, and imagination to the feasting experience, bringing about one of a kind and important contributions for visitors.

The idea of supportability has additionally saturated the universe of extravagance accommodation, affecting the way to deal with culinary development. Extravagance foundations progressively underscore mindful obtaining of fixings, squander decrease, and earth cognizant practices. A few lavish inns and resorts have their own ranches or plants, guaranteeing an immediate and feasible stockpile of new produce.

The wine and drink programs in extravagance neighborliness are organized with similar degree of accuracy and advancement as the culinary contributions. Master sommeliers curate broad wine records, frequently highlighting interesting vintages and remarkable varietals. Make mixed drinks and high quality refreshments are created with an emphasis on flavor profiles that supplement the eating experience. The collaboration between the culinary and refreshment programs is essential to making an amicable and balanced extravagance eating experience.

The idea of customized eating encounters has gotten some decent forward momentum in extravagance neighborliness. Cooks and culinary groups work intimately with visitors to grasp their inclinations, dietary limitations, and culinary goals. This degree of customization considers the production of custom tailored menus, confidential culinary specialist's tables, and vivid eating encounters custom fitted to the singular inclinations of every visitor.

Extravagance accommodation foundations influence the force of narrating to improve the eating experience. The story might spin around the beginnings of explicit fixings, the motivation behind a specific dish, or the social meaning of a culinary practice. Narrating adds layers of profundity to the feasting experience, encouraging an association between the cafe and the culinary excursion.

The idea of location eating has become inseparable from extravagance neighborliness. Lodgings and resorts in beautiful areas influence their environmental elements to make special feasting encounters. Whether it's an ocean front grill, a mountain ridge outing, or a supper in a noteworthy milestone, the setting turns into a vital piece of the culinary story, upgrading the general feeling of extravagance and eliteness.

Extravagance accommodation stretches out its obligation to culinary development past the conventional eatery setting. Room administration, a staple of inn cordiality, is rethought with an emphasis on connoisseur contributions and customized contacts. In-room eating encounters might incorporate confidential gourmet expert administrations, organized tasting menus, and intuitive cooking classes, bringing the extravagance feasting experience straightforwardly to the visitor's doorstep.

The job of the cake and treat gourmet specialist is raised in extravagance neighborliness, with an emphasis on making palatable masterpieces that act as the fantastic finale to the eating experience. Pastries are not simply sweet endings; they are articulations of innovativeness, frequently including mind boggling plating, vanguard procedures, and surprising flavor mixes. The cake kitchen turns into a domain of development and creative mind.

Extravagance cordiality foundations put a top notch on the preparation and improvement of culinary ability. Culinary groups are frequently made out of gifted experts who go through ceaseless preparation to keep up to date with the most recent strategies, patterns, and advancements. This obligation to greatness reaches out to all parts of the eating experience, guaranteeing a consistent and phenomenal experience for visitors.

The idea of culinary homes, where famous gourmet experts take brief home in an extravagance foundation, has acquired notoriety. During these residencies, gourmet experts make unique menus, have intuitive occasions, and deal visitors the chance to encounter their culinary vision firsthand. Culinary homes add a component of eliteness and fervor to the eating scene, drawing in food fans from around the world.

While culinary development in extravagance neighborliness is commended for its imagination and richness, it isn't resistant to challenges. The sensitive harmony among custom and advancement, the interest for consistency across different areas, and the strain to consistently surpass assumptions can present critical difficulties for culinary groups in extravagance foundations. Furthermore, the effect of outside factors, like worldwide occasions or monetary movements, may impact the way to deal with culinary development.

Chapter 5

Unveiling Exclusive Amenities

In the domain of extravagance living, the idea of eliteness takes on another aspect, rising above the traditional limits of lavishness. It is inside this worldview that the thought of divulging restrictive conveniences arises as a significant component in the story of renowned living spaces. The cutting edge knowing occupant looks for a home as well as an encounter — a territory that goes past the customary and raises the idea of home to an unrivaled level.

At the core of this change in perspective is the acknowledgment that conveniences assume a urgent part in characterizing the person and allure of a private turn of events. Gone are the days when a very much designated entryway and a housetop pool were adequate to recognize a top of the line property. Today, engineers and planners are pushing the limits of extravagance, presenting a large group of selective conveniences that take special care of the multi-layered needs and wants of their insightful customers.

One of the vital drivers behind this pattern is the comprehension that extravagance is an emotional and developing idea. What might have been viewed as extreme 10 years prior can now be seen as standard, inciting designers to enhance and reclassify the boundaries of selectiveness constantly. In this mission for differentiation, the uncovering of restrictive conveniences turns into an incredible asset, not exclusively to draw in expected purchasers yet in addition to set another benchmark in the serious scene of extravagance land.

One such select convenience that has acquired unmistakable quality as of late is the confidential film. Distant from the customary thought of a home theater, these confidential films are intended to repeat the loftiness of a conventional film lobby inside the bounds of a home. From best in class sound frameworks to state of the art projection innovation, everything about fastidiously created to give a vivid true to life experience. Velvet draperies separating to uncover a monstrous screen, specially crafted seating, and encompassing lighting that adjusts to the state of mind of the film — all add to an unrivaled survey experience that rises above the customary.

Notwithstanding confidential films, the idea of health and spa conveniences has additionally become the dominant focal point in the domain of selectiveness. Past the standard exercise center and pool, occupants of very good quality advancements can now enjoy spa medicines, steam rooms, and even contemplation gardens — all inside the bounds of their home. The joining of health conveniences mirrors a developing consciousness of the significance of a comprehensive way of life, where physical and mental prosperity are focused on.

One of the characterizing elements of these selective conveniences is their tailor made nature. Engineers are progressively teaming up with prestigious originators and designers to make conveniences that are useful as well as show-stoppers. The custom plan stretches out past the tasteful to the usefulness, guaranteeing that each component is custom fitted to the exceptional inclinations of the inhabitants. This degree of customization adds an individual touch to the living experience, hoisting it from a simple home to an organized magnum opus.

The pattern of selective conveniences isn't restricted to the inside spaces of a home. The outside regions, frequently thought to be as an expansion of the living space, are likewise going through a change. Roof lounges, boundlessness pools with stunning perspectives, and finished gardens are currently normal highlights in extravagance advancements. These open air spaces are intended for style as well as are organized to make a vivid encounter that supplements the general way of life of the occupants.

An arising pattern inside the domain of selective conveniences is the coordination of brilliant home innovation. Past the standard home computerization frameworks, engineers are integrating state of the art innovation that adjusts to the way of life of the inhabitants. From voice-actuated controls to man-made consciousness that learns and expects the inclinations of the tenants, these savvy home frameworks reclassify the idea of accommodation and extravagance. The joining of innovation stretches out to security also, with cutting edge reconnaissance frameworks and biometric access guaranteeing the wellbeing and protection of the occupants.

One more aspect of selectiveness lies in the culinary contributions inside these turns of events. Past the standard kitchen, occupants can now get to private gourmet specialists, organized feasting encounters, and, surprisingly, elite associations with famous cafés. The thought is to give a gastronomic excursion that supplements the refined preferences of the inhabitants, transforming each feast into an important encounter.

The idea of eliteness stretches out past the actual conveniences to the administrations gave inside these turns of events. Individual attendant services, all day, every day security, and valet stopping are presently viewed as standard, however engineers are going above and beyond by offering way of life attendant services. These administrations go past the traditional to take special care of the one of a kind inclinations and wants of the occupants, whether it's organizing a personal luxury plane for an unconstrained escape or getting reservations at the best occasions in the city.

The disclosing of selective conveniences isn't simply a showcasing procedure however a reaction to the developing assumptions for the cutting edge extravagance buyer. In a time where encounters are esteemed as much as assets, these conveniences act as a door to a way of life that rises above the conventional.

They are a demonstration of the possibility that a home isn't simply an actual space yet a material for organized encounters that mirror the uniqueness and goals of its tenants.

Nonetheless, the quest for eliteness isn't without its difficulties. As engineers endeavor to outperform each other in the race for the best conveniences, there is a gamble of surrendering to a need to feel superior mindset. The risk lies in failing to focus on the pith of extravagance living — making spaces that improve the personal satisfaction for the occupants. Engineers really should figure out some kind of harmony among development and common sense, guaranteeing that the elite conveniences are a scene as well as enhance the existences of the occupants.

In addition, the meaning of restrictiveness is emotional and can fluctuate significantly among various socioeconomics. While some might focus on a confidential film, others might esteem a best in class rec center or a devoted space for their specialty assortment. Engineers should remain sensitive to the different inclinations of their interest group and designer their contributions likewise. The critical lies in understanding that selectiveness is definitely not a one-size-fits-all idea however a range that envelops a horde of inclinations and ways of life.

In the journey for selectiveness, supportability is arising as a key thought. The cutting edge extravagance buyer is progressively aware of the natural effect of their decisions, and this mindfulness stretches out to their decision of home. Engineers are answering by coordinating eco-accommodating advancements and plan standards into their turns of events. From sunlight based chargers to green rooftops and energy-proficient frameworks, manageability is presently not a reconsideration yet a key part of restrictive conveniences.

The topographical area of these improvements likewise assumes a significant part in forming the story of eliteness. A home with restrictive conveniences set against the background of a lively city horizon offers an alternate allure contrasted with one settled in a detached regular territory. The environmental elements, whether metropolitan or rustic, add to the general insight and way of life that the improvement offers. Designers are utilizing the special qualities of every area to make a story that lines up with the yearnings of their main interest group.

As the pattern of disclosing select conveniences keeps on advancing, it brings up significant issues about the eventual fate of extravagance living. Will there be an immersion point where each possible convenience has been offered, and designers are constrained to return to the essentials of what comprises genuine selectiveness? Or on the other hand will the quest for development and uniqueness lead to a ceaseless pattern of presenting progressively excessive conveniences?

One likely road for what's to come is the mix of virtual and expanded reality advancements into the living experience. Envision a home where inhabitants can step into a virtual world for a morning exercise or go to a show from the solace of their family room.

The limits between the physical and virtual domains could obscure, opening up additional opportunities for organized encounters that go past the limitations of the actual space.

One more angle to consider is the advancing meaning of extravagance itself. As cultural qualities and inclinations change, the idea of extravagance is probably going to go through a change. It might as of now not be characterized exclusively by material belongings and excessive conveniences yet by encounters that add to individual prosperity, social associations, and a feeling of direction. Engineers who perceive and adjust to this shift will be strategically set up to rethink the account of extravagance living in the years to come.

All in all, the revealing of selective conveniences in the domain of extravagance living addresses a dynamic and developing scene. It is a demonstration of the changing goals and assumptions for the cutting edge extravagance customer, who looks for a home as well as an organized way of life. From private films and wellbeing spas to savvy home innovation and custom plan, these conveniences are molding the account of selectiveness in the serious universe of extravagance land.

As engineers keep on pushing the limits of development, finding some kind of harmony among scene and substance is fundamental. The genuine proportion of progress lies in the loftiness of the conveniences as well as in their capacity to upgrade the personal satisfaction for the occupants. Whether it's a housetop relax with all encompassing perspectives or a maintainable, eco-accommodating.

5.1 Beyond the Ordinary

In the domain of human experience, there exists an enduring longing to rise above the normal, to go after something past the unremarkable and the ordinary. This yearning, profoundly implanted in the human mind, drives people to look for encounters, conditions, and ways of life that go past the conventional. The quest for the phenomenal, the excellent, and the unpredictable turns into a directing power, molding the decisions in different features of their lives.

One of the fields where this mission for the uncommon shows most unmistakably is in the domain of imagination. Whether in artistic expression, sciences, or some other field, the human drive to enhance, to make something that outperforms the normal, is a demonstration of the unlimited idea of human potential. It is in the demonstration of creation that people track down a material to communicate their special viewpoints, pushing the limits of what is viewed as customary or schedule.

This drive to go past the common isn't bound to special goals alone; it reaches out to the manner in which individuals draw in with their general surroundings. From individuals decisions in their regular routines to the conditions they decide to occupy, there is a steady propensity of a craving for uniqueness, for a takeoff from the ordinary.

This tendency is clear in the manner individuals plan their living spaces, curate their ways of life, and search out encounters that surprise everyone.

With regards to living spaces, the idea of "past the common" is progressively forming the scene of structural and inside plan. Property holders and engineers the same are moving past the regular, investigating creative plans and materials that reclassify the thought of a living space. The period of cutout homes is giving way to another rush of structural imagination, where every home is a custom creation, an impression of the uniqueness and goals of its inhabitants.

In the engineering domain, this takeoff from the customary is obvious in the ascent of whimsical designs that challenge conventional ideas of structure and capability. Structures with undulating veneers, structures that consistently mix with the regular scene, and plans that focus on maintainability and eco-kind disposition are turning out to be progressively normal. The point isn't simply to make cover however to create a vivid and unmistakable living experience that reverberates with the ethos of the people who possess these spaces.

In addition, the idea of past the standard stretches out to the inside plan of these spaces. The period of nonexclusive, efficiently manufactured furnishings and stylistic layout is giving way to an interest for custom, handmade pieces that recount a story. Property holders are searching out craftsmans and planners who can make exceptional components that add an individual touch to their living spaces. The normal is supplanted by the uncommon, where each piece has a story, an association with the individual or the way of life from which it exudes.

The longing to rise above the customary isn't restricted to actual spaces alone; it pervades the manner in which individuals approach their ways of life. Individuals decisions with regards to design, travel, and relaxation exercises are progressively directed by a quest for uniqueness and realness. The ascent of specialty and distinctive brands in the style business, for instance, is a reaction to a developing interest for dress and frill that go past efficiently manufactured, conventional contributions. Buyers are searching out pieces that recount to a story, that mirror a guarantee to craftsmanship and uniqueness.

Essentially, in the domain of movement, the mission for encounters past the common is reshaping the travel industry. The ascent of experiential travel, where the actual excursion turns into the objective, is a demonstration of the craving for vivid and capricious encounters. From remaining in treehouses in the core of the wilderness to leaving on social submersion trips in distant towns, explorers are progressively shunning regular vacationer locations for encounters that test and enhance their viewpoints.

The cordiality business is likewise seeing a change driven by the craving to go past the normal. Extravagance resorts and inns are not generally characterized exclusively by rich goods and luxurious conveniences; all things being equal, there is a developing accentuation on giving exceptional and valid encounters.

From submerged lodgings to facilities in reused verifiable structures, the point is to offer visitors a stay that rises above the standard and has an enduring effect.

The idea of past the standard isn't simply bound to actual spaces and encounters; it reaches out to the domain of scholarly and profound investigation. The quest for information, the mission for self-improvement, and the investigation of groundbreaking thoughts are appearances of the human drive to go past the conventional. In the scholar and expert circles, people look for potential open doors that challenge their keenness, permitting them to contribute in significant ways and have an enduring effect.

Moreover, the craving to rise above the common is personally attached to the quest for importance and satisfaction. People are progressively scrutinizing the conventional markers of accomplishment and bliss, creating some distance from a straight direction directed by cultural standards. The normal way of schooling, vocation, and family is being reconsidered for a more all encompassing and individualized way to deal with life. Ideas, for example, balance between serious and fun activities, care, and reason driven living are acquiring unmistakable quality as people look for a more significant association with their reality.

In the domain of connections there is a detectable shift towards associations that go past the customary. The customary ideal models of kinship, family, and heartfelt organizations are developing to oblige a more different and nuanced comprehension of human associations. People are looking for connections that offer realness, common development, and a common feeling of direction — connections that head past cultural assumptions and customary standards.

The computerized age, with its immense range of virtual spaces and stages, has likewise assumed a critical part in molding the mission for past the conventional. Online entertainment, for example, has given people a stage to communicate their extraordinary personalities and interface with similar people across the globe. It has turned into a device for the intensification of different voices and points of view, testing the homogeneity that can once in a while describe customary media.

In any case, chasing past the normal, there are additionally expected traps to explore. The steady mission for curiosity and uniqueness can prompt a feeling of fretfulness, where people are ceaselessly looking for the following unprecedented experience without completely valuing the present. The strain to stick out and be extraordinary can likewise add to insecurities and uneasiness, as people contrast themselves with organized accounts of achievement and satisfaction.

Additionally, the accentuation on the phenomenal can now and again eclipse the excellence and meaning of the standard minutes throughout everyday life.

The commonplace, the daily schedule, and the ordinary encounters are basic to the human experience, and a persistent quest for the unprecedented may bring about a deficiency of appreciation for the effortlessness and legitimacy of these minutes.

In the realm of plan and design, the push for uniqueness can in some cases lead to illogical or impractical arrangements. Finding some kind of harmony among advancement and usefulness is pivotal to guarantee that past the conventional doesn't compare to past the plausible. Likewise, in the mission for exceptional encounters, there is a requirement for dependable the travel industry and a regard for the networks and conditions that have these remarkable experiences.

Notwithstanding these difficulties, the yearning to go past the common remaining parts a strong and extraordinary power. It is an impetus for development, a driver of individual and cultural development, and a wellspring of motivation that impels people to go after new levels. The craving to rise above the common is a festival of the human soul, an affirmation that there is generally space for investigation, disclosure, and the quest for a day to day existence that resounds with legitimacy and importance.

As the world proceeds to advance and people explore the intricacies of the cutting edge period, the idea of past the normal will probably keep on forming the manner in which individuals live, work, and communicate. It is a call to embrace variety, to celebrate singularity, and to develop a mentality that values encounters, connections, and thoughts that go past the bounds of the customary. In the embroidery of human life, the string of the remarkable weaves an account that is rich, dynamic, and particularly private — a consistently unfurling story of people going after the exceptional in the excursion of life.

5.2 Private Spas and Wellness Retreats

Chasing comprehensive prosperity and a definitive getaway from the burdens of current life, a pattern has arisen that rises above the customary spa experience. The idea of private spas and wellbeing withdraws has become the dominant focal point, offering people a cozy and customized asylum where they can revive their body, psyche, and soul. These selective retreats go past the normal spa visit, giving a case of serenity and fitted health encounters that take care of the special necessities and wants of every visitor.

The quintessence of private spas and wellbeing withdraws lies in their capacity to make a separated sanctuary, a space eliminated from the hurrying around of regular daily existence. Not at all like conventional spas that might be clamoring with movement, confidential retreats are intended to offer a feeling of eliteness and serenity. The actual idea of these retreats suggests a takeoff from the standard, welcoming visitors to step into a climate where time dials back, and the center moves completely to taking care of oneself and revival.

One of the characterizing highlights of private spas and wellbeing withdraws is the accentuation on customization. Dissimilar to business spas that might offer normalized medicines, these selective retreats focus on fitting each part of the experience to the singular inclinations and wellbeing objectives of the visitor. From customized health conferences to tailor made treatment designs, each component is created to address the special requirements of the individual, guaranteeing a really groundbreaking and restoring experience.

The actual spaces of private spas and wellbeing withdraws are carefully intended to establish an amicable and relieving climate. Building components, inside plan, and normal environmental elements are undeniably considered to add to a feeling of serenity. The objective is to lay out a consistent association between the fabricated climate and the regular world, encouraging a tranquil environment that improves the general wellbeing experience.

Notwithstanding the actual spaces, the decision of area assumes a pivotal part in molding the personality of private spas and wellbeing withdraws. Large numbers of these retreats are arranged in beautiful and detached settings, encompassed ordinarily's magnificence. Whether settled in the mountains, sitting above the sea, or encompassed in rich backwoods, the picked areas are necessary to the general insight, giving a background that improves the feeling of getaway and association with nature.

The scope of wellbeing contributions at private spas and retreats stretches out a long ways past the conventional spa menu. While back rubs and facials remain staples, these retreats frequently coordinate a different exhibit of health modalities. From comprehensive treatments, for example, Ayurveda and customary Chinese medication to state of the art medicines like cryotherapy and tangible hardship, visitors are given a menu of choices to address their particular wellbeing objectives.

Yoga and reflection are habitually focal parts of private spas and health withdraws. The accentuation on care and mental prosperity lines up with the more extensive change in cultural mindfulness towards all encompassing wellbeing. Retreats might offer confidential meetings with experienced teachers, directed reflection rehearses, and vivid studios to assist visitors with developing a more profound association with their internal identities and encourage a feeling of equilibrium.

Sustenance is one more fundamental part of the health experience at private retreats. Numerous foundations team up with nutritionists and culinary specialists to make tweaked dinner designs that line up with the singular's dietary inclinations and health goals. The spotlight isn't just on giving supporting and heavenly cooking yet additionally on teaching visitors about the job of nourishment in their general prosperity.

The vivid idea of private spas and health withdraws frequently stretches out past the treatment rooms to incorporate wellness and sporting exercises. From private wellness classes and nature climbs to water sports and experience outings, visitors have the valuable chance to take part in exercises that advance actual essentialness and a feeling of experience.

The objective is to give a comprehensive health experience that envelops unwinding as well as revival and rejuvenation.

Innovation likewise assumes a part in upgrading the wellbeing contributions at private retreats. A few foundations integrate progressed wellbeing innovations, like biofeedback gadgets, computer generated reality reflection, and customized wellbeing checking. These developments mean to furnish visitors with bits of knowledge into their prosperity and engage them to play a functioning job in their wellbeing process.

The protection and selectiveness of these retreats stretch out to the actual facilities. Visitors frequently stay in lavish confidential manors or suites furnished with conveniences that go past the standard. Confidential pools, all encompassing perspectives, and customized steward administrations add to a climate of lavishness and segregation. The thought is to make a usual hangout spot where visitors can completely loosen up and drench themselves in the health experience.

Past the physical and experiential perspectives, confidential spas and health withdraws frequently consolidate instructive parts. Studios, talks, and one-on-one meetings with health specialists give visitors information and apparatuses to proceed with their prosperity process past the length of their visit. This instructive aspect adds profundity to the retreat insight, engaging visitors to pursue informed decisions about their wellbeing and way of life.

The prominence of private spas and health retreats can be credited to a conversion of cultural patterns. The rising consciousness of the significance of prosperity, combined with a craving for novel and groundbreaking encounters, has provoked an interest for wellbeing contributions that rise above the customary. The contemporary individual looks for unwinding as well as an extensive and customized way to deal with wellbeing that envelops the physical, mental, and close to home aspects.

As people wrestle with the burdens of present day life, the allure of withdrawing to a confidential desert garden for devoted taking care of oneself has turned into a convincing suggestion. The vivid and customized nature of private spas and health withdraws offers a break from the commotion of day to day existence, permitting visitors to recalibrate and focus on their wellbeing and prosperity. It addresses a cognizant decision to put time and assets in one's wellbeing, recognizing that genuine abundance lies in the condition well.

In any case, the idea of private spas and wellbeing withdraws isn't without its contemplations. The eliteness and extravagance related with these retreats might make them out of reach to a more extensive segment. The test lies in tracking down ways of democratizing health, guaranteeing that the advantages of customized and vivid prosperity encounters are not restricted to a special minority.

Another thought is the requirement for capable and supportable practices inside the health business. As the interest for private spas and retreats develops, there is an obligation to guarantee that these foundations work in an earth cognizant way, regarding the environments wherein they are arranged. This incorporates economical structure rehearses, careful asset utilization, and a promise to supporting nearby networks.

Additionally, the adequacy of private spas and health withdraws is dependent upon people effectively taking part in their wellbeing process. A retreat can give an extraordinary encounter, however the drawn out influence relies upon the singular's obligation to incorporating wellbeing rehearses into their regular routines. Teaching visitors about manageable and feasible wellbeing propensities is vital to guaranteeing that the advantages persevere past the retreat insight.

All in all, confidential spas and health withdraws address a change in outlook in the manner in which people approach prosperity. The accentuation on selectiveness, customization, and a comprehensive way to deal with wellbeing takes special care of the developing inclinations of the cutting edge person. As the health business keeps on growing, confidential retreats act as safe-havens where people can get away, restore, and leave on an excursion towards a more adjusted and satisfying life. Whether settled in tranquil normal scenes or offering state of the art wellbeing innovations, these retreats give a space to people to go past the customary and focus on their wellbeing and prosperity in a groundbreaking and profoundly private manner.

5.3 Personalized Concierge Services

In the domain of extravagance living, the idea of customized attendant services has arisen as a characterizing component that goes past customary thoughts of comfort and administration. Custom fitted to the singular inclinations and requirements of knowing clients, customized attendant services have turned into an essential part of top of the line private encounters, extravagance travel, and restrictive way of life the board. This development mirrors a more extensive change in shopper assumptions, where the quest for custom and organized encounters outweighs normalized contributions.

At the center of customized attendant services is the obligation to conveying a raised and individualized insight. Customarily connected with lodgings and friendliness, attendant services have risen above their beginnings to turn into a diverse and fundamental element in the realm of extravagance. Whether with regards to a confidential home, a top of the line lodging, or an extravagance travel schedule, the customized attendant is situated as a committed facilitator, coordinating a consistent and custom-made insight for the client.

In the private circle, customized attendant services have turned into a sign of selective living. Past the standard contributions of an attendant work area, these administrations stretch out to a domain of modified encounters that take special care of the novel inclinations of inhabitants. From organizing private occasions and tying down selective reservations to overseeing family staff and directing support, the customized attendant turns into a focal figure in upgrading the personal satisfaction inside very good quality homes.

One of the key credits that put customized attendant services aside is the profundity of understanding that attendant experts have about the inclinations, propensities, and way of life of their clients. This information is obtained through continuous connections and a guarantee to expecting the requirements of the client. Dissimilar to conventional attendant services that might zero in on responsive help, the customized approach is proactive, planning to surpass assumptions by prudently tending to prerequisites and arranging tailor made encounters.

The extent of customized attendant services inside private settings reaches out to a different scope of contributions. Occupants might profit from admittance to restrictive occasions, confidential shopping encounters, and organized social trips. The attendant turns into a channel for interfacing occupants with an organization of extravagance suppliers, guaranteeing that each part of their way of life is described by selectiveness and tender loving care.

Besides, the customized attendant is in many cases associated with making customized health encounters for occupants. This might incorporate planning private wellness meetings, orchestrating spa medicines, and coordinating health withdraws. The objective is to make an all encompassing and balanced living experience that lines up with the wellbeing and health objectives of the occupants.

With regards to extravagance travel, customized attendant services assume an essential part in raising the movement experience from the conventional to the unprecedented. Voyagers looking for a custom tailored and vivid excursion frequently connect with the administrations of a committed travel attendant who can coordinate everything about their schedule. This incorporates convenience and transportation as well as customized encounters, confidential visits, and admittance to selective occasions.

The movement attendant turns into an essential accomplice, utilizing their insight into the objective and their organization of contacts to make a movement experience that mirrors the distinction and inclinations of the client. This might include getting reservations at Michelin-featured eateries, orchestrating private admittance to social milestones, or coordinating exceptional and off in an unexpected direction outings. The objective is to make a movement story that goes past the standard and reverberates with the client's yearnings and interests.

The development of customized attendant services in the movement area lines up with the more extensive pattern of experiential travel. Present day extravagance explorers look for something beyond rich facilities; they need significant and credible encounters that have an enduring effect. The movement attendant turns into a guardian of these encounters, guaranteeing that each snapshot of the excursion is portrayed by uniqueness and eliteness.

The approach of innovation has additionally intensified the abilities of customized attendant services. Portable applications, virtual attendant stages, and computerized reasoning driven frameworks empower clients to get to attendant services readily available. These computerized interfaces not just smooth out correspondence among clients and attendant experts yet additionally work with constant updates, suggestions, and reservations.

In the domain of way of life the executives, customized attendant services reach out past private and travel spaces to become thorough answers for people carrying on with requesting and complex existences. High-total assets people, chiefs, and VIPs frequently draw in way of life attendant services to deal with a bunch of undertakings, from sorting out occasions and overseeing family staff to organizing complex schedules and directing individual tasks.

The way of life attendant fills in as a trusted and discrete partner, exploring the intricacies of the client's life and reducing the weight of calculated subtleties. This might include planning personal luxury planes, overseeing selective participations, and organizing a schedule of customized encounters. The objective is to give a consistent and tranquil way of life that permits the client to zero in on their expert and special goals.

The interest for customized attendant services inside the way of life the board circle is demonstrative of a social shift towards reevaluating non-center liabilities. In a period where time is a premium and people look for productivity in each part of their lives, the offer of having a devoted attendant to deal with bunch undertakings is obvious. It isn't just about rethinking undertakings yet about entrusting those assignments to experts who comprehend the subtleties of extravagance living and the assumptions for high-total assets people.

One of the main traits of customized attendant services is the accentuation on carefulness and privacy. Clients who benefit these administrations frequently put a superior on security, and the attendant turns into a confided in partner. The capacity to explore the complexities of the client's life, handle delicate data, and keep an elevated degree of prudence is vital in building and supporting long haul connections.

The progress of customized attendant services depends on the nature of the connections produced between attendant experts and their clients. Not at all like value-based connections, these connections are based on a groundwork of trust, understanding, and a common obligation to surpassing assumptions.

The customized attendant becomes a specialist organization as well as a way of life accomplice, receptive to the subtleties of the client's inclinations and devoted to improving each feature of their life.

While customized attendant services take care of the requirements of high-total assets people, chiefs, and VIPs, there is a continuous work to democratize components of this extravagance experience. A few stages and organizations are investigating ways of making parts of customized attendant services open to a more extensive crowd through membership models or layered help contributions. This democratization tries to expand the advantages of customized help to a more extensive segment while as yet keeping a level of selectiveness for premium levels.

All in all, customized attendant services have developed from a customary idea of cordiality help to turn into a sign of extravagance living, travel, and way of life the board. The accentuation on customization, carefulness, and proactive help recognizes customized attendant services from their ordinary partners. Whether coordinating custom encounters inside very good quality homes, arranging elite travel schedules, or dealing with the intricacies of a client's way of life, the customized attendant fills in as an impetus for lifting each part of the client's life from the common to the remarkable. The proceeded with development of these administrations mirrors a social shift towards a more nuanced and individualized way to deal with extravagance, where the spotlight isn't simply on belongings however on organized encounters and a daily routine very much experienced.

5.4 Cutting-Edge Technological Features

In the unique scene of present day residing, state of the art mechanical elements have turned into a groundbreaking power, reshaping the manner in which people communicate with their surroundings, homes, and day to day schedules. The steady speed of mechanical headway has led to developments that improve accommodation as well as rethink the idea of brilliant, associated, and savvy living spaces. From homes outfitted with best in class computerization frameworks to working environments consolidating the most recent in expanded reality, the combination of state of the art innovation has turned into a sign of contemporary residing.

Brilliant homes, furnished with a plenty of mechanical elements, address a change in outlook in private residing. The idea of home robotization has developed past essential functionalities to envelop a comprehensive biological system where different gadgets flawlessly speak with one another to improve proficiency, security, and solace. Vital to this change is the Web of Things (IoT), an organization of interconnected gadgets implanted with sensors, programming, and different innovations that empower them to trade information and speak with one another.

One of the principal parts of state of the art innovation in savvy homes is home computerization frameworks. These frameworks permit inhabitants to control different parts of their homes from a distance, giving phenomenal comfort and adaptability.

From changing lighting and temperature to overseeing security frameworks and home diversion, the capacity to control and screen the home climate through a cell phone or other savvy gadgets has turned into a standard element in state of the art homes.

Voice-enacted menial helpers, controlled by man-made consciousness (computer based intelligence), have arisen as a focal component in the UI of shrewd homes. Gadgets like Amazon's Alexa, Google Collaborator, and Apple's Siri empower clients to control savvy home gadgets, seek clarification on pressing issues, and get data through voice orders. The incorporation of regular language handling and AI calculations upgrades the abilities of these remote helpers, permitting them to grasp setting, learn client inclinations, and give customized reactions.

Past the fundamental functionalities of home robotization, state of the art homes consolidate progressed security frameworks that influence computer based intelligence and AI. Facial acknowledgment innovation, biometric access controls, and brilliant reconnaissance frameworks improve the security stance of present day homes. AI calculations investigate examples of conduct, permitting the framework to recognize routine exercises and potential security dangers, furnishing occupants with an elevated feeling of safety and control.

The pattern of state of the art innovation reaches out past the private circle to reclassify the idea of the working environment. Brilliant workplaces influence trend setting innovations to make dynamic, responsive, and cooperative workplaces. Expanded reality (AR) and computer generated reality (VR) advancements, for example, empower vivid and intuitive encounters, changing the conventional office space into a center point of development and inventiveness.

Cooperation apparatuses outfitted with state of the art innovation work with consistent correspondence and collaboration among scattered groups. Video conferencing frameworks, virtual whiteboards, and cooperative report altering stages upgrade network and efficiency, empowering experts to cooperate paying little heed to geological areas. The incorporation of artificial intelligence controlled highlights, for example, voice acknowledgment and regular language handling, further smoothes out correspondence and data trade.

The coming of shrewd urban communities addresses an aggregate work to bridle state of the art innovation to work on metropolitan living. These urban communities influence interconnected gadgets, sensors, and information investigation to upgrade proficiency, manageability, and the general personal satisfaction for occupants. Keen transportation frameworks, for instance, use continuous information to streamline traffic stream, lessen blockage, and upgrade public transportation administrations.

Manageability is a vital thought in the improvement of shrewd urban communities, and state of the art innovation assumes an essential part in accomplishing natural objectives.

Brilliant energy matrices, outfitted with sensors and mechanization, advance energy dispersion, diminish wastage, and work with the coordination of environmentally friendly power sources. Squander the board frameworks use IoT sensors to screen and improve squander assortment courses, adding to additional feasible metropolitan environments.

The medical services area has seen a significant effect from state of the art mechanical highlights, with developments that upgrade patient consideration, finding, and therapy. Telemedicine, fueled by cutting edge correspondence advancements, empowers far off conferences and medical services conveyance. Wearable gadgets furnished with wellbeing checking sensors give ongoing information, enabling people to proactively track and deal with their wellbeing.

The reconciliation of artificial intelligence and AI in medical services works with more precise diagnostics and customized therapy plans. Prescient examination models break down huge datasets to distinguish designs, anticipate illness results, and improve treatment systems. Advanced mechanics, outfitted with simulated intelligence calculations, aid medical procedures, recovery, and routine errands, enlarging the abilities of medical care experts and working on tolerant results.

The instruction area has likewise embraced state of the art innovation to change conventional learning conditions. Intuitive smartboards, increased reality applications, and virtual learning stages give understudies vivid and connecting with instructive encounters. Simulated intelligence driven versatile learning frameworks customize instructive substance in light of individual understudy progress, fitting the opportunity for growth to address assorted issues and learning styles.

Blockchain innovation, known for its decentralized and secure nature, has tracked down applications past digital currency in different areas. In finance, blockchain empowers straightforward and carefully designed exchanges, lessening the gamble of extortion and upgrading security. Production network the executives benefits from blockchain's capacity to give a changeless record of exchanges, guaranteeing straightforwardness and recognizability.

State of the art innovation has reformed media outlets, forming how people consume and interface with media. Web-based features, empowered by fast web and high level pressure calculations, offer on-request admittance to an immense library of content. Computer generated reality (VR) and increased reality (AR) innovations make vivid gaming encounters, obscuring the lines between the virtual and genuine universes.

The auto business has gone through an innovative renaissance, with state of the art highlights changing the driving experience. Associated vehicles furnished with IoT sensors give constant information on traffic, climate, and street conditions.

High level driver-help frameworks (ADAS) influence sensors and cameras to upgrade wellbeing, with elements, for example, path keeping help, versatile voyage control, and computerized stopping.

Electric and independent vehicles address the front of development in the car area. Electric vehicles (EVs) influence state of the art battery innovation to give manageable and effective transportation arrangements. Independent vehicles, outfitted with sensors, radar, and simulated intelligence calculations, expect to reclassify portability by lessening the requirement for human mediation and further developing generally speaking street security.

The combination of state of the art innovation has not been without difficulties and contemplations. Protection concerns, network safety gambles, and moral ramifications are among the basic issues that go with the quick speed of innovative headway. The assortment and examination of tremendous measures of individual information bring up issues about information security, client assent, and the expected abuse of data.

Guaranteeing inclusivity and keeping away from the worsening of existing cultural differences is one more thought in the organization of state of the art innovation. The computerized partition, portrayed by differences in admittance to innovation and advanced proficiency, stays a test that should be addressed to guarantee that the advantages of mechanical progression are open to all fragments of society.

Also, the speed of mechanical advancement frequently exceeds administrative systems and moral rules. Finding some kind of harmony between cultivating advancement and laying out capable administration systems is really difficult for policymakers, industry pioneers, and the more extensive society. Moral contemplations encompassing artificial intelligence, computerization, and information security require nonstop discourse and cooperative endeavors to foster structures that protect individual privileges and cultural qualities.

All in all, state of the art mechanical elements have become vital to the texture of present day life, saturating each aspect of society, from homes and working environments to urban areas and enterprises. The extraordinary force of innovation has reshaped how people live, work, and interface with the world. The continuous development of state of the art innovation keeps on introducing valuable open doors and difficulties, requiring an insightful and versatile way to deal with saddle its true capacity to improve society. As innovation keeps on propelling, the direction of its effect will be molded by the aggregate choices made by people, associations, and policymakers, at last deciding the future scene of the computerized age.

Chapter 6

The World of High-End Accommodations

The domain of top of the line facilities is a captivating embroidery woven with strings of extravagance, lavishness, and unrivaled help. In this exceptional world, where everything about carefully organized to make a vivid and extraordinary experience, one leaves on an excursion past simple friendliness; it is an investigation of the great. From the transcending high rises of metropolitan cities to the isolated retreats settled in nature's hug, top of the line facilities reclassify the actual thought of extravagance.

At the core of this domain lies the idea of eliteness. Top of the line facilities are not simply places to rest one's head; they are safe-havens of honor and refinement, saved for the individuals who look for a raised way of life. The engineering of these foundations reflects the magnificence inside, with smooth lines, cutting edge plans, and a consistent mix of current feel and immortal class.

As one stages through the impressive entry of these safe houses of complexity, an orchestra of tangible pleasures starts to unfurl. The climate is painstakingly created to inspire a feeling of tranquility and extravagance. From the delicate murmur of quiet music to the unobtrusive scent that penetrates the air, each component is organized to cover visitors in a universe of extravagance.

The actual facilities are works of art of configuration, including customized decorations, cutting edge innovation, and rich materials that talk about craftsmanship at its pinnacle. Rooms and suites are not just spaces to possess yet are articulations of the craft of residing, where each corner recounts an account of perfect taste and scrupulousness.

In the realm of top of the line facilities, eating is a tangible excursion that rises above the standard. Michelin-featured cafés inside these foundations are gastronomic sanctuaries, where culinary virtuosos make palatable ensembles that dance on the taste buds. The menus are a festival of the best fixings, frequently obtained from around the globe, and the culinary chemists in the background weave sorcery with their mastery.

However, the plushness doesn't stop at the feasting table. Top of the line facilities offer a plenty of sporting and health encounters, guaranteeing that each second is improved with opportunities for revival and self-disclosure.

Luxurious spas, furnished with the most recent treatments and master specialists, entice visitors into a domain of serenity. Wellness focuses rival proficient preparation offices, and open air exercises range from golf on fastidiously manicured courses to water sports in confidential bays.

The mindful and expectant assistance is the sign of top of the line facilities. Staff individuals are not simply representatives; they are craftsmans of neighborliness, adroit at the fragile dance of addressing needs before they are voiced. Customized administrations, from head servant help to custom schedules, take care of the exceptional inclinations of every visitor, guaranteeing that each stay is a consistent and vital experience.

Past the actual domain of these facilities lies a computerized scene where innovation flawlessly coordinates with the specialty of friendliness. Shrewd rooms outfitted with instinctive controls permit visitors to fit their current circumstance as they would prefer, from changing lighting and temperature to getting to theater setups with a basic touch. Virtual attendant services expand the span of customized help, giving data and help at the visitor's fingertips.

The charm of top of the line facilities reaches out past the bounds of the actual space. It entwines with the actual objective, making a cooperative connection between the foundation and its environmental elements. Whether roosted on the edge of a precipice with all encompassing perspectives or tucked away in the core of a clamoring city, these facilities become basic to the story of the district.

The obligation to manageability and ecological cognizance is a developing feature of top of the line facilities. Ground breaking foundations are embracing eco-accommodating practices, from energy-proficient innovations to privately obtained and natural materials. The point isn't simply to give an extravagant encounter however to do as such with a careful and dependable methodology that regards the planet.

As day gives way to night in the realm of top of the line facilities, the environment goes through a groundbreaking movement. Bars and parlors wake up with the clunking of glasses and the mumble of discussions, causing a cozy and complex social situation. Mixologists create signature mixed drinks, and sommeliers guide visitors through basements supplied with intriguing vintages, guaranteeing that each drink is a toast to refinement.

Unique occasions and festivities become extraordinary issues in the possession of the proficient occasion organizers related with these facilities. From weddings that rival regal services to corporate social affairs executed with accuracy, these foundations consistently mix magnificence with usefulness. Every occasion is a material whereupon dreams are painted, with the setting of extravagance upgrading the scene.

In the realm of top of the line facilities, the idea of time itself goes through a change. It turns into a liquid element, where minutes are extended and relished.

The surge of the rest of the world is abandoned, and visitors are welcome to thrive in the present. It is a domain where breakfast can be delighted in at recreation, where daily can unfurl without a foreordained timetable, and where the straightforward demonstration of unwinding turns into a work of art.

The appeal of top of the line facilities stretches out to the universe of business and business venture. These foundations act as scenes for high-stakes gatherings, restrictive meetings, and systems administration occasions where arrangements of monstrous size are facilitated. The consistent combination of business and extravagance establishes a climate helpful for development and coordinated effort, where the limits among work and relaxation obscure.

In the background, the tasks of top of the line facilities are an expressive dance of accuracy and coordination. A devoted group works enthusiastically to guarantee that each visitor experience is perfect, from the neatness of the rooms to the quickness of room administration. The kitchens are centers of inventiveness, where culinary maestros organize an ensemble of flavors, and the attendant work area is a nexus of data and help.

The universe of top of the line facilities isn't safe to the unavoidable trends. As cultural qualities advance, so too do the assumptions for knowing explorers. Variety and inclusivity become indispensable contemplations, and foundations endeavor to establish conditions that invite visitors from varying backgrounds. Social responsiveness and a promise to social obligation become core values, molding the ethos of these sanctuaries of extravagance.

The eventual fate of very good quality facilities is an enticing possibility, with development as its compass. Headways in innovation, economical practices, and configuration will keep on rethinking the scene. The mission forever vivid encounters will prompt the reconciliation of virtual and expanded reality, permitting visitors to rise above the actual bounds of the foundation and leave on virtual undertakings.

The development of private and elite travel encounters will additionally hoist the idea of extravagance. From personal luxury plane contracts to tailor made schedules organized by movement specialists, the insightful voyager will approach a universe of potential outcomes. Very good quality facilities will reach out past conventional lodgings, with private manors, yachts, and, surprisingly, far off extravagance camps becoming sought-after safe houses for those in quest for the remarkable.

The worldwide scene of very good quality facilities is a mosaic of different impacts. Every area contributes its novel flavor to the embroidery, mirroring the social subtleties and building feel of the district. From the moderate polish of Japanese ryokans to the luxurious wonder of Center Eastern royal residences, top of the line facilities draw motivation from the rich legacy of the spots they possess.

All in all, the universe of very good quality facilities is a domain where extravagance rises above the material and turns into a vivid encounter. It is a reality where each sense is uplifted, and each second is a chance for guilty pleasure. From the fastidiously planned spaces to the customized administration, these foundations reclassify the actual substance of neighborliness.

As the sun sets not too far off and projects a brilliant gleam over the very good quality facilities dispersed across the globe, one is left with a significant appreciation for the imaginativeness that goes into making these sanctuaries of refinement. Whether it's an end of the week retreat, a celebratory occasion, or a business rendezvous, these foundations coax with the commitment of an uncommon excursion — an excursion into the universe of very good quality facilities where extravagance exceeds all logical limitations.

6.1 Luxurious Suites and Villas

In the domain of lavish facilities, sumptuous suites and estates stand as the encapsulation of plushness and eliteness. These safe houses of guilty pleasure rethink the idea of neighborliness, offering knowing explorers a sample of the uncommon. From stylish metropolitan suites to rambling confidential estates settled in unspoiled scenes, these safe-havens take special care of the people who look for a spot to remain as well as a vivid encounter where everything about a demonstration of refined residing.

The appeal of sumptuous suites starts with the actual plan of these spaces. Modelers and inside originators team up to establish conditions that consistently mix contemporary feel with ageless class. The outcome is many times an agreeable combination of smooth lines, vanguard goods, and customized components that add to a feeling of complexity. From the second one stages through the entryway, a feeling of glory envelopes the visitor, making way for a remarkable stay.

The actual facilities are show-stoppers of solace and style. Rich decorations, premium textures, and cautiously organized fine art add to an air of guilty pleasure. Top of the line materials like marble, silk, and intriguing woods are regularly utilized, for their lavish allure as well as for the material joy they give. The room turns into a safe-haven of serenity, embellished with rich cloths and decorated with insightful contacts like customized conveniences and encompassing lighting.

The idea of customized administration becomes the overwhelming focus in extravagant suites. Devoted attendant services guarantee that each impulse and want is expected and satisfied. From organizing restrictive encounters to getting difficult to come by things, the attendant turns into a believed partner in making a tailor made stay. The coordination of innovation further improves the visitor experience, with brilliant frameworks controlling all that from lighting and temperature to in-room diversion.

Eating in lavish suites is an encounter regardless of anyone else's opinion. Confidential gourmet experts, knowledgeable in the culinary expressions, make customized menus custom-made to the visitor's inclinations. In-room eating rises above the everyday, turning into a gastronomic excursion where each dish is a show-stopper. The cautiously organized wine and spirits determination guarantees that each taste is a toast to refinement, delighted in the protection of one's own sumptuous territory.

The appeal of private manors lies in the sweeping retreat they give. Settled in detached settings, these manors frequently brag stunning perspectives on regular scenes, be it flawless sea shores, rich mountains, or moving grape plantations. The engineering of these retreats is a marriage of neighborhood impacts and contemporary plan, making a feeling of spot that is both true and rich.

The insides of private manors are intended to inspire a feeling of home, though an outstandingly luxurious one. Roomy living regions, completely prepared kitchens, and various rooms take special care of those looking for a private encounter. Confidential pools, gardens, and outside relaxing regions obscure the lines among indoor and open air residing, making a comprehensive retreat where visitors can luxuriate surrounded by wealth and excess while drenched in nature.

Security is vital in the realm of private estates. High walls, lavish finishing, and circumspect doors guarantee that visitors can partake it might be said of disconnection. The devoted manor staff works with the greatest possible level of prudence, offering mindful support while regarding the visitor's requirement for isolation. For the individuals who esteem selectiveness, confidential estates become a shelter where time dials back, and the rest of the world disappears.

The culinary encounters in confidential estates are no less extreme. Confidential cooks curate dinners utilizing the freshest nearby fixings, making a gastronomic excursion that mirrors the kinds of the district. Visitors have the adaptability to eat at their favored time, whether it's a relaxed breakfast on the porch or a candlelit supper under the stars. The eating experience turns into a festival of both culinary creativity and the regular environmental elements.

Sporting conveniences in confidential manors are intended for the people who look for both unwinding and experience. Confidential spa medicines, wellness focuses, and open air exercises organized by committed manor staff take care of the changed interests of the visitors. Whether it's a directed climb through neighboring paths, a confidential yoga meeting at the crack of dawn, or a day of water sports on a confined ocean side, the opportunities for relaxation are basically as different as the inclinations of the insightful explorer.

Administration in confidential manors goes past the customary; it is a movement of expectant signals and smart contacts. Estate directors coordinate each part of the stay, from pre-appearance inclinations to sorting out custom tailored encounters.

The staff, from servants to private gourmet specialists, turns into a fundamental piece of the visitor's excursion, guaranteeing that each second is taken care of with the most elevated level of care.

The advancement of sumptuous suites and confidential estates mirrors the changing inclinations of the cutting edge explorer. Maintainability and eco-cognizant practices have become fundamental contemplations in the plan and activity of these facilities. Ground breaking foundations integrate energy-productive innovations, privately obtained materials, and eco-accommodating drives, adjusting the quest for extravagance to a guarantee to natural obligation.

The fate of extravagant facilities is ready at the convergence of innovation and customized administration. Savvy rooms furnished with manmade brainpower expect and take special care of the visitor's inclinations, establishing a climate that adjusts to individual requirements. Virtual attendant services, increased reality encounters, and consistent mix of innovation into the visitor venture are not too far off, promising another time of vivid extravagance.

The worldwide scene of lavish suites and confidential manors is a material painted with different impacts. Every objective contributes its novel person, from the smooth metropolitan retreats in clamoring cities to the natural stylish manors in peaceful wide open settings. The ongoing idea, nonetheless, is the steadfast obligation to giving an unrivaled visitor experience, where extravagance isn't simply a condition of being nevertheless an excursion into the remarkable.

All in all, the universe of sumptuous suites and confidential manors addresses a zenith of friendliness where each component, from plan to support, is raised to a fine art. These facilities are not simply places to remain; they are vivid encounters that wait in the memory long after the excursion has finished. Whether it's the stylish class of a metropolitan suite or the separated extravagance of a confidential manor, these shelters of guilty pleasure entice the people who look for the exceptional, welcoming them into an existence where extravagance has no limits.

6.2 Opulent Bedrooms and Lavish Bathrooms

In the realm of extravagance facilities, rich rooms and sumptuous restrooms stand as safe-havens of solace and guilty pleasure. These confidential spaces go past simple usefulness; they are carefully planned safe houses that raise the idea of rest and revival to an artistic expression. From luxurious textures to custom decorations, from state of the art innovation to spa-like conveniences, these rooms and restrooms are created to give a vivid encounter that rises above the conventional.

The lavishness of rooms in extravagance facilities is quickly clear in their plan and stylistic layout. Modelers and inside fashioners team up to make spaces that wed stylish allure with usefulness.

The outcome is in many cases an amicable mix of contemporary plan components and immortal style. From the second one enters, the air oozes a feeling of refinement, making way for a serene and extravagant stay.

Key to the appeal of extravagant rooms is the actual bed. In extravagance facilities, the bed isn't simply a household item; it is a lofty position of rest. Rich cloths, extravagant cushions, and top notch beddings guarantee a tranquil night's rest. The selection of materials stretches out past simple solace; it addresses a guarantee to quality and a commitment to giving the highest level of in extravagance. From the string count of the sheets to the selection of pads, everything about considered.

Goods in lavish rooms are cautiously organized to upgrade both structure and capability. From custom tailored closets to complicatedly planned end tables, each piece is chosen to add to the general stylish. The utilization of lavish materials like hardwoods, metals, and fine textures adds to the material joy of the space. The room turns into a casing of solace, welcoming visitors to loosen up in a climate that is however outwardly engaging as it seems to be unwinding.

Lighting assumes an essential part in making the ideal climate in lavish rooms. Specially crafted installations, encompassing lighting choices, and insightful situation add to a space that can be custom fitted to suit different states of mind. Whether it's the delicate sparkle of bedside lights for a comfortable night read or decisively positioned recessed lighting to feature compositional subtleties, the lighting plan in extravagance rooms is a painstakingly coordinated dance of brightening.

Innovation consistently incorporates into extravagant rooms, upgrading the visitor experience. Shrewd frameworks control all that from lighting and temperature to diversion choices. Computerized draperies and blinds permit visitors to easily change the degree of normal light, establishing a customized and agreeable climate. Top of the line general media frameworks, including huge screen TVs and encompass sound, add a diversion layer to the room, changing it into a sight and sound sanctuary.

The idea of the in-room attendant further hoists the visitor experience in extravagant rooms. Devoted staff individuals are accessible to take special care of the all visitor's requirements, from organizing customized encounters to guaranteeing that the room is supplied with favored conveniences. The in-room attendant turns into a contact between the visitor and the heap contributions of the extravagance convenience, guaranteeing that each solicitation is met with the most elevated level of administration.

Connecting rich rooms, the en-suite washrooms are an orchestra of extravagance and usefulness. In these sumptuous spaces, the restroom isn't simply a utilitarian need however a retreat inside a retreat.

The plan of these restrooms is a marriage of feel and common sense, highlighting premium materials, best in class installations, and smart designs that upgrade the general visitor experience.

The highlight of these extravagant restrooms is much of the time the detached bath. Situated decisively to expand sees or decorated with sensational lighting, these tubs become more than simple installations; they are sculptural components that welcome visitors to enjoy a tranquil washing experience. Very good quality materials like marble and cleaned stone add to the sumptuous mood, changing the restroom into a confidential spa.

The shower insight in extravagant washrooms is similarly debauched. Stroll in showers with precipitation showerheads, steam choices, and flexible settings take care of individual inclinations. The utilization of premium tiling, consistent glass nooks, and custom equipment makes a spa-like climate. High level water control frameworks permit visitors to customize the temperature and strain, guaranteeing a tweaked and liberal shower insight.

The selection of materials in lavish washrooms reaches out past feel to incorporate a promise to supportability and eco-cognizant practices. Extravagance facilities are progressively consolidating harmless to the ecosystem materials, water-saving apparatuses, and energy-proficient advances in their restroom plans. The accentuation on supportability mirrors a developing consciousness of the natural effect of extravagance living and a longing to offset lavishness with capable practices.

Washroom conveniences in rich facilities are a smart expansion of the general insight. Very good quality toiletries, frequently from lofty brands, are painstakingly chosen to improve the tactile joy of the visitor. From scented shower salts to lavish body salves, these conveniences add to a spa-like encounter inside the bounds of the confidential restroom. The tender loving care in giving premium items highlights the obligation to offering a far reaching extravagance experience.

Mirrors, one more fundamental component of restroom configuration, are many times treated as enlivening elements in extravagant facilities. Specially crafted mirrors with incorporated lighting add a hint of excitement while filling a useful need. Reflected walls or broad reflected surfaces make a deception of room, intensifying the feeling of extravagance. The cautious position of mirrors likewise permits visitors to appreciate shocking perspectives while approaching their preparing customs.

The mix of innovation in luxurious washrooms reaches out to highlights like warmed floors, shrewd mirrors with worked in shows, and high level sound frameworks. Cutting edge latrines with elements like warmed seats, worked in bidets, and adaptable settings further improve the feeling of extravagance. The consistent mix of innovation into washroom configuration mirrors a guarantee to development and a longing to furnish visitors with the most recent conveniences.

The format of lavish washrooms is intended to expand space and make a feeling of receptiveness. Separate vanity regions, frequently furnished with specially crafted cupboards and more than adequate capacity, take care of the necessities of visitors. The insightful arrangement of mirrors and lighting guarantees that the prepping and it are sufficiently bright and useful to dress regions. The general plan supports a consistent stream between various components, establishing a strong and outwardly satisfying climate.

All in all, rich rooms and extravagant restrooms in extravagance facilities rethink the craft of accommodation. These confidential spaces are not only places to rest; they are vivid conditions that take special care of the faculties and hoist the visitor experience to unmatched levels. From the cautiously organized decorations in the room to the spa-like conveniences in the restroom, everything about a demonstration of a guarantee to extravagance living. As voyagers look for encounters that go past the conventional, rich rooms and luxurious washrooms stand as safe-havens that offer a retreat into a reality where solace, style, and extravagance merge.

6.3 Tailored In-Room Experiences

In the consistently developing scene of extravagance facilities, customized in-room encounters arise as a characterizing component that goes past the customary idea of friendliness. These custom tailored contributions are carefully organized to take care of the novel inclinations and wants of every visitor, changing a stay into a vivid excursion that reflects individual preferences and desires. From customized conveniences to organized social encounters, the universe of fitted in-room encounters is a demonstration of the responsibility of extravagance facilities to make extraordinary minutes for their visitors.

At the core of custom fitted in-room encounters lies the idea of personalization. Gone are the times of one-size-fits-all accommodation; all things considered, the emphasis is on creating encounters that resound with the particular necessities and wants of every visitor. This shift is driven by an acknowledgment that insightful explorers look for more than simple solace; they want an association with the objective and a feeling of genuineness that goes past the surface.

One of the critical components of customized in-room encounters is the idea of pre-appearance inclinations. Extravagance facilities, outfitted with booking ahead of time frameworks and visitor profiles, endeavor to comprehend the singular preferences of their benefactors before they even step through the entryway. From room temperature settings to the selection of pads, these inclinations are noted and carried out to guarantee that the visitor feels invited as well as really comprehended.

A foundation of custom fitted in-room encounters is the arrangement of tailor made conveniences. These go past the standard contributions to incorporate things and administrations that line up with the visitor's way of life.

Whether it's a most loved brand of toiletries, an arranged choice of bites and refreshments, or customized wellness hardware, these conveniences are painstakingly chosen to establish a climate that feels like a usual hangout spot.

The reconciliation of innovation assumes a significant part in conveying customized in-room encounters. Savvy room frameworks permit visitors to control different parts of their current circumstance with a dash of a button or a voice order. From changing the lighting to setting the room temperature, these mechanical developments give a consistent and instinctive way for visitors to fit their environmental factors as per their inclinations.

Custom-made in-room encounters stretch out past the actual space to incorporate a scope of organized administrations. Confidential feasting encounters, coordinated by prestigious cooks, bring the culinary expressions straightforwardly to the visitor's room. From private meals to celebratory events, these customized eating choices permit visitors to enjoy connoisseur food in the solace and protection of their own space. Wine and soul tastings, with master sommeliers directing the experience, further lift the in-room culinary excursion.

The idea of in-room wellbeing encounters is acquiring conspicuousness in extravagance facilities. Confidential spa medicines, from back rubs to facials, are arranged to take special care of individual inclinations. Gifted specialists bring the reviving advantages of spa treatments straightforwardly to the visitor's room, considering a customized and vivid health experience. Yoga teachers and wellness mentors are likewise available to give private meetings, guaranteeing that visitors can keep up with their health schedules in the protection of their convenience.

The social setting of the objective assumes a huge part in forming custom-made in-room encounters. Extravagance facilities influence their nearby associations with offer visitors a more profound drenching into the objective's legacy and customs. Whether it's a confidential visit drove by a learned aide, an organized workmanship assortment that mirrors the nearby culture, or in-room encounters that grandstand territorial craftsmanship, these contributions make a feeling of spot that goes past the shallow.

For those looking for scholarly feeling, customized in-room encounters might incorporate admittance to an organized library of books, narratives, or talks custom-made to the visitor's advantages. Craftsmanship fans might find their room decorated with painstakingly chosen works of art or even have the chance to take part in confidential viewings with a nearby craftsman. These custom fitted social contributions guarantee that visitors can enjoy their interests and interests without leaving the solace of their convenience.

The job of the in-room attendant is fundamental to the outcome of custom-made encounters. These devoted experts act as the visitors' very own contacts, arranging each part of their visit.

From orchestrating elite trips to organizing in-room festivities, the in-room attendant turns into a believed partner in making a consistent and customized insight. Their insight into the objective, combined with a comprehension of the visitor's inclinations, considers the curation of encounters that are both extraordinary and essential.

Festivities and unique events become remarkable undertakings with the help of in-room attendants. Whether it's an achievement birthday, a commemoration, or a heartfelt escape, these experts work in the background to guarantee that everything about immaculately executed. From orchestrating customized designs and shock gifts to planning tailor made feasting encounters, the in-room attendant changes festivities into minutes that will be treasured for a lifetime.

The idea of fitted in-room encounters reaches out to the universe of business and corporate travel. Extravagance facilities perceive the novel requirements of business voyagers and look to offer customized types of assistance that take special care of both work and unwinding. In-room office arrangements, rapid web, and admittance to business administrations guarantee that visitors can flawlessly direct their expert undertakings while partaking in the solace and extravagance of their convenience.

The reconciliation of virtual attendant services further improves the visitor experience by giving moment admittance to data and help. Through intuitive stages and portable applications, visitors can investigate arranged suggestions for feasting, amusement, and social encounters. Virtual attendant services consider constant correspondence with the in-room attendant, guaranteeing that any solicitation or question can be tended to immediately, upgrading the general degree of administration.

As manageability turns into an undeniably huge thought in the realm of extravagance travel, custom-made in-room encounters are lining up with eco-cognizant practices. From eco-accommodating conveniences and privately obtained items to energy-effective advancements, facilities are coordinating maintainable components into their contributions. This mirrors a more extensive obligation to mindful extravagance, recognizing the ecological effect of movement and endeavoring to limit it.

Planning ahead, the scene of custom fitted in-room encounters is ready for additional advancement. Propels in man-made reasoning and AI are supposed to improve the personalization of visitor encounters. Prescient calculations might expect visitor inclinations in light of past ways of behaving, making a degree of administration that isn't simply responsive however expectant. Virtual and expanded reality may likewise assume a part in drenching visitors in customized virtual conditions or improving in-room diversion choices.

All in all, customized in-room encounters address a change in outlook in the realm of extravagance facilities. These tailor made contributions go past the traditional limits of cordiality, perceiving that insightful explorers look for in excess of a brief getaway — they look for a customized venture that reverberates with their singularity. From organized conveniences to in-room health encounters, these custom-made contributions make a feeling of association, guaranteeing that visitors feel invited as well as genuinely comprehended. As extravagance facilities keep on developing, the craft of fitting in-room encounters remains as a demonstration of the obligation to giving unrivaled snapshots of delight, solace, and guilty pleasure.

6.4 Privacy and Security in Five-Star Residences

In the domain of extravagance living, the ideas of protection and security take on elevated significance, especially with regards to five-star homes. These select dwelling places, whether settled in the core of a clamoring city or roosted on the quiet shores of a detached objective, are intended to give lavishness as well as a safe-haven of protection and a stronghold of safety. The combination of state of the art innovation, careful preparation, and cautious administrations guarantees that occupants of these five-star homes experience a degree of protection and security that is unrivaled.

Protection in five-star homes stretches out past the simple actual limits of the property; it envelops a comprehensive way to deal with defending the individual space and character of the occupants. Design assumes a critical part in establishing a climate that offers separation without settling on feel. High walls, lavish finishing, and vital arrangement of designs are utilized to safeguard the home from inquisitive eyes, encouraging an environment of restrictiveness.

Namelessness is a valued part of security in five-star homes. Inhabitants, frequently people of unmistakable quality or those looking for a careful way of life, esteem the capacity to move about their homes and normal regions without unjustifiable consideration. Plan contemplations, like confidential passageways and circumspect vehicular access, are carried out to work with the consistent development of inhabitants while protecting their secrecy.

High level security frameworks are coordinated consistently into the texture of five-star homes to furnish inhabitants with a feeling of consolation. Cutting edge reconnaissance cameras, biometric access controls, and shrewd sensors add to an extensive security foundation. The utilization of facial acknowledgment innovation further upgrades access control, guaranteeing that main approved people can enter the premises.

Confidential security faculty, frequently prepared to the best expectations, are a noticeable presence in five-star homes. These experts are entrusted with actual security as well as go about as attendant level staff, prepared to expect and address the necessities of inhabitants. Their prudent presence adds an additional layer of affirmation, and their capacity to mix away from plain sight embodies the obligation to saving the private climate.

The obligation to security reaches out to the computerized domain in five-star homes. Online protection measures are executed to shield occupants' very own information, guaranteeing that mechanical frameworks, from shrewd home gadgets to individual correspondence organizations, are safeguarded against unapproved access. With the rising predominance of shrewd home advancements, inhabitants anticipate that their associated gadgets should be secure, and extravagance homes focus on hearty network protection measures to live up to these assumptions.

Five-star homes frequently highlight private lifts that open straightforwardly into the inhabitants' residing spaces. This improves comfort as well as adds an additional layer of safety by restricting admittance to assigned floors. Inhabitants can move easily from the hall to their homes without experiencing normal passageways or shared spaces, further adding to the feeling of isolation.

Finishing and open air plan are basic parts of security in five-star homes. Confidential nurseries, housetop porches, and segregated outside spaces are painstakingly wanted to offer occupants an association with nature without settling for less on protection. High supports, decisively positioned trees, and water highlights add to a serene outside climate protected from outer perspectives.

An elevated degree of protection likewise reaches out to the plan of individual homes inside these selective turns of events. Formats are carefully created to guarantee that rooms, individual living spaces, and open air regions are protected from adjoining units. The essential situation of windows, the utilization of soundproofing materials, and creative structural arrangements add to a feeling of isolation inside the actual home.

The universe of five-star homes perceives the significance of caution in assistance conveyance. Occupant demands, whether for in-room feasting, housekeeping, or attendant services, are taken care of with the highest level of secrecy. Staff individuals are prepared to regard the protection of occupants, guaranteeing that their presence is felt just when required and that their activities add to a consistent and inconspicuous living experience.

The idea of protection additionally reaches out to the social spaces inside five-star homes. Restrictive parlors, confidential feasting regions, and common spaces are intended to encourage a feeling of local area among occupants while regarding their requirement for individual space. Get-togethers and social occasions are organized with circumspection, permitting occupants to draw in with their neighbors in a way that lines up with their inclinations.

In the realm of five-star homes, the harmony among protection and local area is a fragile dance. While inhabitants esteem isolation, they additionally look for open doors for social association inside the bounds of their restrictive living climate.

Normal regions, for example, spa offices, wellness focuses, and relax, are intended to work with socialization while giving confidential corners to the people who favor isolation.

Security in five-star homes is a complex undertaking that envelops both physical and mechanical viewpoints. Monitored security designated spots, furnished with the most recent screening advancements, are frequently situated at the passages to guarantee that main approved people get entrance. Security work force go through thorough preparation to deal with a scope of circumstances, from crisis reaction to guaranteeing the everyday wellbeing of inhabitants.

Getting the borders of five-star homes includes a mix of actual obstructions and cutting edge innovation. High walls or fencing, frequently tactfully coordinated into the finishing, give a visual obstacle, while electronic reconnaissance frameworks and sensors go about as a proactive guard. The objective is to make a solid territory that occupants can call home, realizing that their security is a first concern.

Five-star homes focus on the security of inhabitants during both constantly. Sufficiently bright pathways, secure stopping regions, and all day, every day monitored security add to a solid climate. What's more, the arrangement of cutting edge access control frameworks, like key cards or biometric examines, guarantees that main approved people can enter the premises at some random time.

The idea of smart security is acquiring noticeable quality in extravagance homes. Brilliant home advances are utilized to upgrade security, permitting inhabitants to remotely screen and control different parts of their home. Coordinated alert frameworks, movement sensors, and ongoing video observation give occupants genuine serenity, realizing that their home is furnished with state of the art security highlights.

Secure stopping offices are an essential part of safety in five-star homes. Underground or committed leaving regions with controlled admittance furnish inhabitants with a protected space for their vehicles. The joining of reconnaissance cameras and normal watches guarantees the security of occupants and their property inside these assigned parking spots.

In case of a crisis, five-star homes focus on a quick and effective reaction. Crisis reaction plans, including clearing methods and coordination with nearby specialists, are set up to address a scope of circumstances. Inhabitants approach every minute of every day crisis administrations, and the presence of prepared faculty guarantees a fast and powerful reaction to any security-related occurrences.

The mix of safety with attendant services is a sign of five-star homes. The security work force frequently twofold as attendant staff, giving a consistent mix of wellbeing and administration.

Whether helping with transportation plans, taking care of conveyances, or giving data, these experts add to a climate where security is consistently woven into the texture of day to day existence.

Mechanical headways assume a pivotal part in guaranteeing the security of occupants in five-star facilities. Biometric access frameworks, including unique mark or retina examines, add an additional layer of insurance to passage focuses. Robotized tag acknowledgment frameworks and savvy reconnaissance cameras furnished with facial acknowledgment innovation add to thorough safety efforts.

Five-star homes likewise perceive the significance of establishing a safe climate for kids and families. Youngster amicable safety efforts, like secure play regions, checked passageways, and prepared staff, guarantee that more youthful occupants can partake in the advantages of extravagance living without settling for less on wellbeing. The attention on family security mirrors the advancing socioeconomics of occupants in these restrictive turns of events.

The idea of protection and security in five-star homes reaches out to the advanced scene. Network protection measures are carried out to defend occupants' private and monetary data. Encoded correspondence channels, secure Wi-Fi organizations, and customary security reviews are important for the complete methodology to shield inhabitants from digital dangers, guaranteeing that their advanced lives are just about as secure as their actual spaces.

All in all, the universe of five-star homes puts a superior on protection and security, perceiving that occupants look for extravagance as well as a safe-haven where they can reside liberated from interruption. The fastidious plan, combination of cutting edge innovation, and cautious administrations aggregately add to a climate that focuses on the prosperity and protection of the people who call these select homes home. As the scene of extravagance living keeps on developing, the accentuation on protection and security stays a steadfast responsibility, guaranteeing.

In the domain of extravagance living, Five-Star Homes stand as strongholds of lavishness, selectiveness, and unrivaled solace. These unprecedented houses reclassify the idea of home, offering occupants a raised way of life that rises above the common. From compositional works of art to customized insides, and from customized administrations to cutting edge conveniences, these homes are created to take care of the most insightful people who look for a spot to reside as well as a vivid encounter that exemplifies the zenith of extravagance.

The compositional plan of Five-Star Homes is in many cases an amicable combination of feel, usefulness, and development. Famous draftsmen team up with visionary designers to make structures that are not only structures but rather milestones.

Whether settled in the core of an energetic city, roosted on a picturesque slope, or encompassed by unblemished nature, these homes are decisively situated to offer stunning perspectives and a feeling of spot that supplements their environmental factors.

The outsides of Five-Star Homes are a visual demonstration of the obligation to greatness. Forcing veneers, fastidious finishing, and tender loving care characterize the initial feeling. The utilization of great materials, from unblemished marble to sparkling glass, mirrors a faithful commitment to making a home that radiates extravagance from each point. The compositional language frequently lines up with the social and verifiable setting of the area, making an interesting character for every home.

Past the outside charm, the insides of Five-Star Homes are organized flawlessly. Famous inside originators are enrolled to change living spaces into show-stoppers. Each component, from the selection of decorations to the choice of craftsmanship pieces, adds to a feeling of refinement. The consistent joining of innovation, tailor made gets done, and careful scrupulousness raise these insides to the embodiment of extravagance living.

The living spaces inside Five-Star Homes are intended to be both fantastic and cozy. Far reaching family rooms with floor-to-roof windows, originator kitchens furnished with first in class machines, and lavish eating regions take special care of occupants who value the better things throughout everyday life. The designs are mindfully intended to expand regular light, sees, and spatial stream, establishing an amicable living climate that is however utilitarian as it seems to be stylishly satisfying.

Rooms in Five-Star Homes are asylums of solace and serenity. Luxurious goods, premium materials, and custom plan components add to an environment of plushness. The joining of brilliant home innovation permits occupants to control lighting, temperature, and diversion with the bit of a button. Stroll in wardrobes, confidential galleries, and en-suite restrooms with spa-like conveniences add to the general feeling of extravagance and accommodation.

The kitchens inside these homes are culinary safe houses furnished with cutting edge apparatuses and hand crafted highlights. Whether occupants are culinary devotees or depend on confidential gourmet specialists, the kitchens are intended to oblige a scope of culinary pursuits. From smooth contemporary plans to immortal works of art, the kitchens in Five-Star Homes are a mix of usefulness and class, giving occupants the best setting for culinary guilty pleasure.

Open air spaces in Five-Star Homes are expansions of the residing experience. Confidential patios, galleries, and roof gardens offer inhabitants the chance to associate with nature while appreciating all encompassing perspectives.

Nicely planned outside relaxing and eating regions give the ideal setting to unwinding or engaging visitors. Finishing is frequently organized to upgrade the regular excellence of the environmental factors, making a consistent progress among indoor and outside living.

A sign of Five-Star Homes is the arrangement of custom tailored administrations that take care of the interesting necessities and wants of occupants. Committed attendant services are accessible nonstop to help with a horde of solicitations, from organizing venture out schedules to getting reservations at selective eateries. The attendant turns into an individual partner, guaranteeing that occupants can zero in on partaking in their way of life without the weight of everyday undertakings.

Security and protection are vital in the realm of Five-Star Homes. Monitored security designated spots, biometric access controls, and modern reconnaissance frameworks add to a far reaching security foundation. The homes are intended to offer a feeling of disengagement, with private passages, secure stopping offices, and tactful vehicular access. Namelessness is esteemed, and gauges are taken to guarantee that inhabitants can move about their living spaces without interruption.

The idea of health is incorporated into the way of life presented by Five-Star Homes. Confidential wellness places furnished with the most recent gym equipment, fitness coaches, and health programs take special care of inhabitants who focus on wellbeing and prosperity. Spa offices, including private treatment rooms, saunas, and unwinding regions, offer a safe-haven for restoration. The all encompassing way to deal with wellbeing mirrors a promise to furnishing occupants with a way of life that supports both body and brain.

Notwithstanding actual health, Five-Star Homes perceive the significance of mental and profound prosperity. Quiet contemplation spaces, yoga studios with all encompassing perspectives, and open air reflection gardens give occupants spaces for thoughtfulness and unwinding. The accentuation on comprehensive health lines up with the developing needs of people looking for a reasonable and agreeable way of life.

Five-Star Homes frequently include select amusement spaces that take care of inhabitants' shifted preferences. Confidential screening rooms with state of the art general media frameworks offer a true to life experience inside the solace of the home. Game rooms, libraries, and workmanship displays give spaces to recreation and social pursuits. The reconciliation of shrewd home innovation permits occupants to tweak their diversion encounters, from making customized playlists to controlling lighting and mood.

The idea of local area is painstakingly sustained inside Five-Star Homes. Restrictive parlors, social spaces, and common regions are intended to work with connection among occupants. Get-togethers, organized by devoted occasion organizers, offer open doors for systems administration and brotherhood.

The feeling of local area reaches out past the actual spaces, with advanced stages and occupant applications encouraging availability and correspondence among inhabitants.

Five-Star Homes frequently highlight private feasting offices that rival the best cafés on the planet. Eminent cooks or catering administrations are enrolled to furnish inhabitants with connoisseur culinary encounters inside the solace of their homes. Whether facilitating private suppers or excellent festivals, inhabitants can partake in a top notch feasting experience without leaving their home. Wine basements with organized determinations add an additional layer of refinement to private feasting encounters.

The idea of maintainability is progressively coordinated into the plan and tasks of Five-Star Homes. From energy-effective advances and eco-accommodating structure materials to feasible arranging rehearses, these homes endeavor to limit their natural effect. The obligation to maintainability mirrors a consciousness of worldwide natural worries and a commitment to dependable living.

The combination of innovation is a characterizing part of the Five-Star Homes insight. Shrewd home frameworks permit occupants to control lighting, temperature, diversion, and security with the bit of a screen or a voice order. High level computerization highlights, like mechanized window medicines and brilliant machines, upgrade accommodation and productivity. The consistent incorporation of innovation is intended to hoist the occupant experience and give a degree of control that lines up with present day living.

The idea of possession in Five-Star Homes frequently reaches out past conventional land models. Fragmentary possession, confidential home clubs, and other creative proprietorship structures offer adaptability and selectiveness. These models permit people to partake in the advantages of extravagance living without the obligations of all year support. The developing scene of proprietorship choices mirrors a longing to take special care of different ways of life and inclinations.

Planning ahead, the universe of Five-Star Homes is ready for proceeded with advancement and development. Progressions in innovation, manageability rehearses, and the joining of health ideas are supposed to shape the up and coming age of extravagance living. The idea of experiential extravagance, where occupants are offered organized encounters that go past material belongings, is probably going to acquire conspicuousness, mirroring a more extensive change in purchaser inclinations toward significant and vivid ways of life.

Chapter 7

Exquisite Entertainment and Events

Perfect Diversion and Occasions embodies the convergence of inventiveness and careful preparation, offering a customized experience that rises above common social events. Established in the way of thinking that each occasion is an extraordinary story holding on to unfurl, the organization has cut a specialty for itself in the serious domain of occasion the executives. From lavish weddings to corporate affairs, Dazzling Diversion and Occasions has excelled at changing dreams into extraordinary real factors.

At the center of their prosperity lies a group of old pros who offer an abundance of involvement and imagination that might be of some value. The excursion starts with a cooperative work to figure out the client's vision, inclinations, and goals. This underlying stage, set apart by open correspondence and a sharp meticulousness, establishes the vibe for the whole occasion arranging process.

One of the signs of Lovely Diversion and Occasions is their obligation to development. In an industry where patterns advance quickly, remaining on top of things is foremost. The group highly esteems its capacity to implant every occasion with new and innovative components that enthrall participants and have an enduring effect. Whether it's a state of the art subject for an item send off or an unconventional idea for a fantasy wedding, Lovely Diversion and Occasions succeeds in pushing the limits of traditional occasion plan.

The fastidious arranging process includes everything from setting choice to catering, amusement, and planned operations. The group explores the maze of potential outcomes with artfulness, guaranteeing that every component consistently meshes into the general story of the occasion.

Meticulousness isn't simply an expression for Stunning Diversion and Occasions; a core value pervades each choice and activity.

As the occasion date draws near, the group's coordination and execution ability come to the front. A very much arranged orchestra of sellers, entertainers, and coordinated operations guarantees that the situation develops immaculately.

Impeccable Amusement and Occasions invests wholeheartedly in its capacity to deal with the complexities of huge scope occasions without settling for less on quality. From organizing with Top notch performers to overseeing celebrity conventions, the group's capability is apparent in the smooth progression of each and every occasion they attempt.

The organization's portfolio traverses a different scope of occasions, each customized to meet the special necessities of its customer base. Weddings, with their innate profound importance, are changed into fantasy encounters that rise above assumptions. Stunning Diversion and Occasions teams up intimately with couples to grasp their romantic tale and make an interpretation of it into a fastidiously organized festival that mirrors their characters.

Corporate occasions, then again, request an alternate arrangement of abilities and contemplations. Wonderful Diversion and Occasions has effectively organized high-profile corporate functions, item dispatches, and meetings, procuring a standing for conveying occasions as well as vital brand encounters. The group grasps the corporate scene and adjusts its methodologies to the client's image personality, making occasions that resound with the interest group.

Widespread developments represent a one of a kind test, requiring a top to bottom comprehension of customs, customs, and responsive qualities. Lovely Amusement and Occasions embraces this variety and use its multicultural ability to make vivid social encounters. From conventional services to current combinations, the group explores the fragile harmony between safeguarding legacy and mixing contemporary energy.

Pledge drives and magnanimous occasions hold an extraordinary spot in Stunning Diversion and Occasions' portfolio. The group perceives the significance of these occasions in making positive social effect. With a sharp comprehension of the fragile subtleties included, they make occasions that strike an agreeable harmony between the reason and the crowd, boosting both mindfulness and raising support potential.

Behind the glamour and style of each and every occasion lies a guarantee to manageability. Flawless Amusement and Occasions embraces eco-accommodating practices and pursues limiting the natural impression of every occasion. From obtaining locally to executing waste decrease gauges, the organization incorporates manageability flawlessly into its occasion arranging ethos.

The progress of Impeccable Diversion and Occasions can be credited not exclusively to its innovative pizazz and careful preparation yet additionally to its relentless obligation to client fulfillment. The group moves toward each task with a cooperative mentality, seeing clients as accomplices in the inventive flow. This cooperative soul cultivates a feeling of trust and straightforwardness, establishing the groundwork for effective and persevering through connections.

In an industry where notorieties are based on verbal, Dazzling Diversion and Occasions has gained notoriety for surpassing assumptions. Tributes from fulfilled clients highlight the organization's devotion to conveying unrivaled encounters. The capacity to reliably meet and outperform client assumptions has situated Lovely Diversion and Occasions as a pioneer in the cutthroat scene of occasion the board.

The powerful idea of the occasion business requests steady variation to arising patterns and innovations. Perfect Diversion and Occasions embraces development as a main impetus, utilizing state of the art innovation to upgrade the general occasion insight. Virtual and crossover occasions, increased reality, and intuitive components are flawlessly incorporated to make vivid and connecting with encounters that rise above actual limits.

The group at Perfect Diversion and Occasions perceives that the outcome of an occasion stretches out past the actual day. Post-occasion assessments and criticism systems are fundamental to the organization's consistent improvement process. This obligation to refinement guarantees that each resulting occasion expands upon the accomplishments of its ancestors, hoisting the norm of greatness with each endeavor.

The cutthroat scene of the occasion business requires a ground breaking way to deal with business improvement. Perfect Amusement and Occasions isn't content to become complacent; all things considered, it effectively looks for new open doors for development and extension. Key organizations, statistical surveying, and a proactive way to deal with industry patterns position the organization as a unique player in a steadily developing scene.

Schooling and information sharing structure a pivotal part of Wonderful Diversion and Occasions' corporate ethos. The group is focused on keeping up to date with the most recent patterns, advancements, and best practices in the business. This responsibility reaches out past interior preparation projects to outside drives, like studios, online classes, and mentorship programs that add to the general development and advancement of the occasion the executives local area.

The worldwide reach of Flawless Diversion and Occasions is a demonstration of its capacity to rise above geological limits. The organization has effectively executed occasions on a global scale, exploring assorted social scenes with artfulness. This worldwide viewpoint grows the organization's customer base as well as enhances its innovative range, mixing a cosmopolitan pizazz into each occasion it embraces.

A guarantee to social obligation is imbued in the DNA of Wonderful Diversion and Occasions. Past making noteworthy encounters, the organization effectively looks for ways of rewarding the local area. Whether through magnanimous occasions, associations with non-benefit associations, or drives that help nearby networks, Stunning Diversion and Occasions endeavors to have a beneficial outcome past the domain of occasion the executives.

The eventual fate of Dazzling Diversion and Occasions is set apart by a proceeded with devotion to greatness and a steady quest for development. The organization imagines itself as a pioneer, setting new guidelines for the occasion business. From spearheading patterns to reclassifying the limits of imagination, Choice Diversion and Occasions tries to be a main impetus that shapes the future scene of occasions on a worldwide scale.

All in all, Flawless Diversion and Occasions remains as a signal of greatness in the realm of occasion the board. Through an amicable mix of innovativeness, careful preparation, and resolute devotion to client fulfillment, the organization has cut a specialty for itself as well as set a benchmark for the business. As it proceeds to develop and embrace the difficulties of a consistently evolving scene, Stunning Diversion and Occasions stays resolute in its obligation to conveying unprecedented encounters that rise above the conventional.

7.1 Grand Celebrations

Stupendous Festivals, an encapsulation of tastefulness and imagination, remains as a robust in the domain of occasion arranging and the board. With a rich embroidery of involvement woven through incalculable fruitful occasions, the organization has secured itself as a signal of development and greatness. From cozy get-togethers to fantastic functions, Excellent Festivals succeeds in transforming dreams into the real world, creating encounters that wait in the hearts and brains of participants long after the occasion finishes up.

At the core of Stupendous Festivals is a group of old pros who offer an abundance of skill that would be useful. The excursion starts with a careful comprehension of the client's vision, inclinations, and goals. This cooperative methodology, set apart by open correspondence and a sharp eye for detail, establishes the groundwork for the whole occasion arranging process.

One of Fantastic Festivals' characterizing highlights is its obligation to pushing the limits of inventiveness. In an industry where patterns develop quickly, the organization values its capacity to implant every occasion with new and creative components that dazzle participants. Whether it's an unusual subject for a birthday festivity or a modern idea for a corporate social occasion, Stupendous Festivals stands apart for its ability to reclassify the principles of occasion plan.

The arranging system at Terrific Festivals is an extensive excursion that envelops everything from scene choice to providing food, diversion, and operations. Exploring this multifaceted scene with artfulness, the group guarantees that every component consistently meshes into the all-encompassing story of the occasion. Tender loving care isn't simply a mantra for Terrific Festivals; a core value saturates each choice and activity.

As the occasion date draws near, the coordination and execution ability of the group come to the very front. A perfectly tuned joint effort of merchants, entertainers, and strategies guarantees that the situation develops immaculately.

Terrific Festivals invests wholeheartedly in its capacity to deal with the complexities of huge scope occasions without settling on quality. From organizing with eminent performers to overseeing celebrity conventions, the group's capability is obvious in the consistent progression of each and every occasion they embrace.

The broad arrangement of Fantastic Festivals traverses a different scope of occasions, each custom-made to meet the remarkable requirements and wants of its customer base. Weddings, with their close to home importance, are changed into captivating encounters that go past assumptions. Excellent Festivals teams up intimately with couples, unwinding their romantic tale and making an interpretation of it into a fastidiously organized festival that mirrors their characters.

Corporate occasions request an alternate arrangement of abilities and contemplations, and Fantastic Festivals has effectively coordinated high-profile celebrations, item dispatches, and gatherings. The group comprehends the corporate scene, adjusting its systems to the client's image character to make occasions that meet business goals as well as have an enduring effect on participants.

Comprehensive developments, with their inborn variety, represent a one of a kind test that Fabulous Festivals embraces sincerely. The group use its multicultural ability to make vivid encounters, from customary functions to current combinations. Exploring the sensitive harmony between safeguarding legacy and imbuing contemporary energy, Fantastic

Festivals has turned into a confided in accomplice for socially rich occasions.

Pledge drives and beneficent occasions possess a unique spot in Fabulous Festivals' portfolio. The group perceives the significance of these occasions in making positive social effect. With a profound comprehension of the subtleties in question, they make occasions that reverberate with the reason and the crowd, expanding both mindfulness and raising money potential.

Manageability is a basic belief for Fabulous Festivals. The organization effectively integrates eco-accommodating practices, from locally obtaining materials to carrying out squander decrease measures. The obligation to maintainability goes past being a pattern; it's a necessary piece of Stupendous Festivals' ethos, adding to a greener and more capable occasion industry.

Client fulfillment isn't simply an objective for Fantastic Festivals; it's a non-debatable norm. The group moves toward each undertaking with a cooperative outlook, seeing clients as accomplices in the inventive strategy. This cooperative soul cultivates trust and straightforwardness, making an establishment for fruitful and persevering through connections. In an industry where notoriety is fundamental, Excellent Festivals' obligation to surpassing assumptions has brought about a flood of positive tributes from fulfilled clients.

In the background, development is a main impetus for Fabulous Festivals. The organization effectively embraces arising advancements to improve the general occasion insight. Virtual and half and half occasions, expanded reality, and intuitive components are flawlessly incorporated, making vivid and connecting with encounters that rise above actual limits.

Post-occasion assessments and input systems are fundamental to Fabulous Festivals' constant improvement process. This obligation to refinement guarantees that each ensuing occasion expands upon the triumphs of its ancestors, lifting the norm of greatness with each endeavor. The organization comprehends that the progress of an occasion reaches out past the actual day, and the gaining from every occasion adds to its development and advancement.

The serious idea of the occasion business requires a ground breaking way to deal with business improvement. Fabulous Festivals effectively looks for new open doors for development and extension. Key organizations, statistical surveying, and a proactive way to deal with industry patterns position the organization as a powerful player in a consistently developing scene.

Training and information sharing are crucial parts of Fabulous Festivals' corporate culture. The group is devoted to keeping up to date with the most recent patterns, advancements, and best practices in the business. This responsibility stretches out past inner preparation projects to outer drives, like studios, online classes, and mentorship programs that add to the general development and improvement of the occasion the executives local area.

The worldwide reach of Terrific Festivals is a demonstration of its capacity to rise above geological limits. The organization has effectively executed occasions on a worldwide scale, exploring different social scenes with artfulness. This worldwide point of view extends the organization's customer base as well as improves its inventive range, implanting a cosmopolitan pizazz into each occasion it embraces.

Social obligation isn't simply a slogan for Excellent Festivals; it's a central rule. Past making vital encounters, the organization effectively looks for ways of rewarding the local area. Whether through magnanimous occasions, associations with non-benefit associations, or drives that help nearby networks, Thousand Festivals endeavors to have a beneficial outcome past the domain of occasion the executives.

The eventual fate of Stupendous Festivals is set apart by a proceeded with commitment to greatness and a constant quest for development. The organization imagines itself as a trailblazer, setting new principles for the occasion business. From spearheading patterns to rethinking the limits of inventiveness, Fantastic Festivals tries to be a main thrust that shapes the future scene of occasions on a worldwide scale.

All in all, Fantastic Festivals remains as a paragon of greatness in the realm of occasion the executives. Through an agreeable mix of imagination, careful preparation, and a resolute obligation to client fulfillment, the organization has cut a specialty for itself as well as set a benchmark for the business. As it proceeds to develop and embrace the difficulties of an always evolving scene, Stupendous Festivals stays enduring in its obligation to conveying unprecedented encounters that rise above the normal.

7.2 Hosting Elite Gatherings

Facilitating Tip top Get-togethers is a vanguard in the circle of occasion arranging and the board, coordinating unmatched encounters that rethink extravagance and refinement. With a distinguished history of organizing uncommon occasions, the organization has secured itself as a trailblazer, pushing the limits of inventiveness and setting new guidelines for world class social events. From selective soirées to high-profile corporate occasions, Facilitating Tip top Get-togethers explores the many-sided embroidery of extravagance with artfulness, guaranteeing that every occasion turns into an indication of the client's vision and yearnings.

The substance of Facilitating Tip top Get-togethers lies in its recognized group of experts, each offering an abundance of involvement and skill that might be of some value. The excursion initiates with an intensive investigation of the client's longings, inclinations, and targets. This cooperative methodology, described by open correspondence and a fastidious comprehension of individual requirements, shapes the bedrock of the whole occasion arranging process.

A central quality of Facilitating First class Social events is its faithful obligation to hoisting the idea of extravagance. In an industry where plushness is the norm, the organization separates itself by mixing every occasion with customized components that encapsulate eliteness. Whether it's a confidential festival in a sumptuous chateau or a corporate function in a lofty scene, Facilitating World class Social events is proficient at making encounters that rise above the common.

The arranging system at Facilitating Tip top Social events is an ensemble of accuracy, including all that from choosing notorious scenes to coordinating consistent operations, and organizing culinary joys that tempt the sense of taste. Exploring this multifaceted excursion with fastidious scrupulousness, the group guarantees that each feature adjusts flawlessly with the general story of the occasion. The quest for flawlessness is certainly not a simple yearning for Facilitating World class Get-togethers; a major rule pervades each choice and activity.

As the occasion date draws near, the group's coordination and execution ability become the dominant focal point. An agreeable cooperation of sellers, specialists, and coordinated operations specialists guarantees that the situation transpires immaculately. Facilitating Tip top Social affairs values the capacity to deal with the intricacies of enormous scope occasions without settling for less on the nature of administration.

From liaising with widely acclaimed entertainers to carrying out celebrity conventions, the group's capability is apparent in the consistent execution of each and every occasion they embrace.

The arrangement of Facilitating Tip top Get-togethers traverses a range of occasions, each custom-made to surpass the assumptions for its tip top customer base. Extreme weddings, described by loftiness and complexity, are changed into fantasy encounters that rise above the limits of creative mind. The organization works together intimately with couples, diving into the complexities of their romantic tale and making an interpretation of it into a fastidiously organized festival that mirrors their special embodiment.

Corporate occasions, a space where accuracy and distinction are vital, are fastidiously organized by Facilitating Tip top Get-togethers. The group comprehends the complexities of the corporate world, adjusting its techniques to the client's image personality to make occasions that meet business goals as well as resound with participants on a significant level.

Comprehensive developments, with their rich embroidery of customs and customs, present a remarkable material for Facilitating First class Social occasions. The group use its social insight to organize vivid encounters, from customary functions to contemporary combinations. Finding some kind of harmony among legacy and innovation, Facilitating World class Social occasions has turned into a confided in accomplice for those looking for socially rich and significant occasions.

Pledge drives and beneficent occasions hold a unique spot in Facilitating First class Social events' collection. The group perceives the cultural effect of such occasions and endeavors to make encounters that bring issues to light as well as contribute considerably to respectable purposes. With a profound comprehension of the subtleties in question, they create occasions that strike the ideal harmony between the reason and the crowd, expanding both effect and raising support potential.

Maintainability isn't simply a popular expression for Facilitating Tip top Get-togethers; it's an essential part of its occasion arranging ethos. The organization effectively coordinates eco-accommodating practices, from obtaining locally to executing waste decrease measures. The obligation to supportability isn't only a sign of approval for latest things; it mirrors a firmly established liability to the climate and a dream for a more maintainable occasion industry.

Client fulfillment isn't only a measurement for Facilitating Tip top Social events; it's a demonstration of its obligation to greatness. The group moves toward each task with a cooperative mentality, seeing clients not only as benefactors yet as accomplices in the inventive flow. This cooperative soul encourages trust and straightforwardness, making an establishment for effective and getting through connections.

In an industry where notoriety is central, Facilitating Tip top Get-togethers' commitment to surpassing assumptions has brought about a nonstop stream of shining tributes from fulfilled clients.

Advancement is the backbone of Facilitating First class Social events. The organization embraces arising advancements to improve the general occasion insight. Virtual and cross breed occasions, increased reality, and intuitive components are flawlessly woven into the texture of its contributions, making vivid and connecting with encounters that rise above the limits of traditional occasions.

Post-occasion assessments and criticism systems are basic to Facilitating World class Get-togethers' obligation to persistent improvement. Gaining from every occasion isn't simply a training; a central rule guarantees each ensuing occasion expands upon the triumphs of its ancestors, increasing present expectations of greatness with each endeavor.

The cutthroat idea of the occasion business requires a ground breaking way to deal with business improvement. Facilitating World class Get-togethers effectively looks for new open doors for development and extension. Vital organizations, statistical surveying, and a proactive position towards industry patterns position the organization as a powerful player in a consistently developing scene.

Instruction and information sharing are crucial mainstays of Facilitating Tip top Get-togethers' corporate culture. The group is committed to remaining at the cutting edge of the most recent patterns, advances, and best practices in the business. This responsibility stretches out past inward preparation projects to envelop outer drives like studios, online classes, and mentorship programs, adding to the general development and advancement of the occasion the executives local area.

The worldwide reach of Facilitating Tip top Social occasions bears witness to its capacity to rise above geological limits. The organization has effectively executed occasions on a global scale, exploring assorted social scenes with artfulness. This worldwide viewpoint expands the organization's customer base as well as improves its imaginative range, mixing a cosmopolitan energy into each occasion it embraces.

Social obligation is woven into the actual texture of Facilitating First class Get-togethers. Past making unprecedented encounters, the organization effectively looks for ways of rewarding the local area. Whether through beneficent occasions, associations with non-benefit associations, or drives that help neighborhood networks, Facilitating First class Get-togethers endeavors to have a constructive outcome that reaches out a long ways past the domain of occasion the executives.

The future of Facilitating Tip top Social events is set apart by a proceeded with devotion to greatness and an unfaltering quest for development. The organization imagines itself as a member as well as a trailblazer, forming the future scene of tip top get-togethers. From spearheading patterns to reclassifying the limits of extravagance, Facilitating World class Get-togethers tries to be a main impetus that sets new benchmarks for the business on a worldwide scale.

All in all, Facilitating Tip top Social affairs remains as an exemplification of greatness in the realm of occasion the board. Through an amicable mix of innovativeness, careful preparation, and an enduring obligation to client fulfillment, the organization has cut a specialty for itself as well as set a highest quality level for the business. As it proceeds to develop and embrace the difficulties of an always evolving scene, Facilitating World class Social affairs stays unflinching in its obligation to conveying uncommon encounters that rise above the conventional.

7.3 Exclusive Events and Entertainment

Select Occasions and Diversion remains as a signal of extravagance and complexity in the powerful domain of occasion arranging and the executives. Famous for coordinating lavish encounters that reclassify the limits of excess, the organization has hardened its situation as a trailblazer, creating occasions that make a permanent imprint on the memory of participants. From selective soirées to high-profile corporate capabilities, Restrictive Occasions and Diversion explores the scene of extravagance with unmatched artfulness, guaranteeing that every occasion turns into an indication of the client's vision and desires.

At the center of Select Occasions and Diversion is a group of old pros, each contributing an abundance of involvement and skill to the organization's collection. The excursion starts with a careful investigation of the client's cravings, inclinations, and goals. This cooperative methodology, portrayed by straightforward correspondence and a far reaching comprehension of individual necessities, establishes the groundwork for the whole occasion arranging process.

An obvious attribute of Selective Occasions and Amusement is its faithful obligation to lifting the idea of extravagance. In an industry where richness is the norm, the organization separates itself by mixing every occasion with custom components that encapsulate selectiveness. Whether coordinating a confidential festival in an extravagant manor or organizing a corporate celebration in an esteemed setting, Restrictive Occasions and Diversion is proficient at making encounters that rise above the common.

The arranging system at Restrictive Occasions and Diversion is a fastidious excursion incorporating all that from choosing famous settings to coordinating consistent operations and organizing culinary enjoyments that entice the sense of taste.

Exploring this complicated embroidered artwork with careful scrupulousness, the group guarantees that each aspect adjusts consistently with the general story of the occasion. The quest for flawlessness is definitely not a simple ideal for Restrictive Occasions and Diversion; a crucial standard penetrates each choice and activity.

As the occasion date draws near, the coordination and execution ability of the group become the overwhelming focus. An amicable cooperation of merchants, craftsmen, and planned operations specialists guarantees that the situation develops perfectly. Selective Occasions and Amusement invests wholeheartedly in its capacity to deal with the intricacies of huge scope occasions without settling for less on the nature of administration. From liaising with widely acclaimed entertainers to carrying out celebrity conventions, the group's capability is clear in the consistent execution of each and every occasion they attempt.

The arrangement of Select Occasions and Diversion traverses a range of occasions, each carefully custom-made to surpass the assumptions for its insightful customer base. Excessive weddings, portrayed by loftiness and complexity, are changed into fantasy encounters that rise above the limits of creative mind. The organization works together intimately with couples, digging into the complexities of their romantic tale and making an interpretation of it into a fastidiously organized festival that mirrors their special substance.

Corporate occasions, a space where accuracy and distinction are central, are fastidiously organized by Elite Occasions and Diversion. The group comprehends the complexities of the corporate world, adjusting its procedures to the client's image character to make occasions that meet business goals as well as resound with participants on a significant level.

Comprehensive developments, with their rich embroidery of customs and customs, present a special material for Select Occasions and Diversion. The group use its social astuteness to organize vivid encounters, from conventional services to contemporary combinations. Finding some kind of harmony among legacy and innovation, Selective Occasions and Diversion has turned into a confided in accomplice for those looking for socially rich and significant occasions.

Pledge drives and beneficent occasions hold an exceptional spot in the collection of Selective Occasions and Diversion. The group perceives the cultural effect of such occasions and endeavors to make encounters that bring issues to light as well as contribute considerably to respectable purposes. With a profound comprehension of the subtleties in question, they make occasions that strike the ideal harmony between the reason and the crowd, boosting both effect and raising support potential.

Supportability isn't simply a brief pattern for Restrictive Occasions and Diversion; it's an essential part of its occasion arranging ethos. The organization effectively incorporates eco-accommodating practices, from obtaining locally to carrying out squander decrease measures.

The obligation to maintainability isn't simply a sign of approval for ebb and flow ecological worries; it mirrors a firmly established liability to the climate and a dream for a more feasible occasion industry.

Client fulfillment isn't only a measurement for Selective Occasions and Diversion; it's a demonstration of its obligation to greatness. The group moves toward each task with a cooperative mentality, seeing clients not simply as benefactors yet as accomplices in the innovative strategy. This cooperative soul cultivates trust and straightforwardness, making an establishment for fruitful and getting through connections. In an industry where notoriety is fundamental, Restrictive Occasions and Diversion's commitment to surpassing assumptions has brought about a persistent stream of gleaming tributes from fulfilled clients.

Advancement is the backbone of Restrictive Occasions and Amusement. The organization embraces arising advancements to improve the general occasion insight. Virtual and crossover occasions, expanded reality, and intuitive components are flawlessly woven into the texture of its contributions, making vivid and connecting with encounters that rise above the limits of traditional occasions.

Post-occasion assessments and input systems are fundamental to Restrictive Occasions and Amusement's obligation to persistent improvement. Gaining from every occasion isn't simply a training; a crucial rule guarantees each resulting occasion expands upon the triumphs of its ancestors, increasing present expectations of greatness with each endeavor.

The cutthroat idea of the occasion business requires a ground breaking way to deal with business improvement. Selective Occasions and Amusement effectively looks for new open doors for development and extension. Vital organizations, statistical surveying, and a proactive position towards industry patterns position the organization as a powerful player in a consistently developing scene.

Instruction and information sharing are principal mainstays of Selective Occasions and Amusement's corporate culture. The group is devoted to remaining at the front line of the most recent patterns, advancements, and best practices in the business. This responsibility stretches out past inner preparation projects to incorporate outer drives like studios, online classes, and mentorship programs, adding to the general development and improvement of the occasion the board local area.

The worldwide reach of Select Occasions and Amusement confirms its capacity to rise above geological limits. The organization has effectively executed occasions on a global scale, exploring assorted social scenes with artfulness. This worldwide viewpoint expands the organization's customers as well as enhances its imaginative range, imbuing a cosmopolitan style into each occasion it embraces.

Social obligation is woven into the actual texture of Restrictive Occasions and Diversion. Past making exceptional encounters, the organization effectively looks for ways of rewarding the local area. Whether through beneficent occasions, associations with non-benefit associations, or drives that help neighborhood networks, Elite Occasions and Diversion endeavors to have a beneficial outcome that stretches out a long ways past the domain of occasion the board.

The fate of Selective Occasions and Diversion is set apart by a proceeded with devotion to greatness and an immovable quest for development. The organization imagines itself as a member as well as an innovator, molding the future scene of select occasions and diversion. From spearheading patterns to rethinking the limits of extravagance, Selective Occasions and Diversion tries to be a main thrust that sets new benchmarks for the business on a worldwide scale.

All in all, Restrictive Occasions and Amusement remains as an exemplification of greatness in the realm of occasion the executives. Through an agreeable mix of innovativeness, fastidious preparation, and an unfaltering obligation to client fulfillment, the organization has cut a specialty for itself as well as set a best quality level for the business. As it proceeds to advance and embrace the difficulties of a consistently evolving scene, Restrictive Occasions and Diversion stays enduring in its obligation to conveying exceptional encounters that rise above the standard.

7.4 Redefining Extravagance in Social Functions

Reclassifying Lavishness in Friendly Capabilities, a pioneer in the domain of occasion arranging and the board, has situated itself as a leading figure for richness and refinement. Prestigious for organizing occasions that rise above the standard, the organization has become inseparable from extravagance and development. From elite soirees to great social capabilities, Reclassifying Excess explores the complicated scene of high-profile occasions with artfulness, making vivid encounters that make a permanent imprint on participants.

At the center of Rethinking Lavishness in Friendly Capabilities is a group of old pros, each contributing an abundance of involvement and imagination to the organization's portfolio. The excursion starts with an extensive investigation of the client's longings, inclinations, and goals. This cooperative methodology, set apart by open correspondence and a careful comprehension of individual requirements, fills in as the establishment for the whole occasion arranging process.

A particular quality of Rethinking Lavishness in Friendly Capabilities is its unflinching obligation to hoisting the idea of excess. In an industry where loftiness is the assumption, the organization separates itself by mixing every occasion with custom components that encapsulate selectiveness. Whether coordinating a confidential festival in a rich domain or organizing a social capability in an esteemed setting, Rethinking Luxury in Friendly Capabilities succeeds at creating encounters that rise above customary standards.

The arranging system at Rethinking Excess in Friendly Capabilities is a careful excursion that envelops all that from choosing famous settings to organizing consistent coordinated operations and organizing culinary show-stoppers that entice the sense of taste. Exploring this many-sided woven artwork with fastidious scrupulousness, the group guarantees that each component adjusts consistently with the all-encompassing account of the occasion. The quest for flawlessness isn't only a yearning for Reclassifying Excess in Friendly Capabilities; a basic standard saturates each choice and activity.

As the occasion date draws near, the coordination and execution ability of the group become the overwhelming focus. An amicable joint effort of sellers, craftsmen, and planned operations specialists guarantees that the situation transpires faultlessly. Reclassifying Lavishness in Friendly Capabilities invests heavily in its capacity to deal with the intricacies of huge scope occasions without settling for less on the nature of administration. From liaising with widely acclaimed entertainers to carrying out celebrity conventions, the group's capability is apparent in the consistent execution of each and every occasion they attempt.

The arrangement of Rethinking Lavishness in Friendly Capabilities traverses a range of occasions, each carefully custom-made to surpass the assumptions for its insightful customer base. Luxurious weddings, portrayed by greatness and refinement, are changed into fantasy encounters that rise above the limits of creative mind. The organization teams up intimately with couples, digging into the complexities of their romantic tale and making an interpretation of it into a fastidiously arranged festival that mirrors their remarkable pith.

Corporate occasions, a space where accuracy and eminence are fundamental, are fastidiously coordinated by Reclassifying Luxury in Friendly Capabilities. The group comprehends the complexities of the corporate world, adjusting its procedures to the client's image personality to make occasions that meet business targets as well as reverberate with participants on a significant level.

Far-reaching developments, with their rich embroidery of customs and customs, present an extraordinary material for Rethinking Excess in Friendly Capabilities. The group use its social sharpness to organize vivid encounters, from customary functions to contemporary combinations. Finding some kind of harmony among legacy and advancement, Rethinking Luxury in Friendly Capabilities has turned into a confided in accomplice for those looking for socially rich and significant occasions.

Pledge drives and beneficent occasions hold an extraordinary spot in the collection of Rethinking Excess in Friendly Capabilities. The group perceives the cultural effect of such occasions and endeavors to make encounters that bring issues to light as well as contribute considerably to honorable goals. With a profound comprehension of the subtleties in question, they make occasions that strike the ideal harmony between the reason and the crowd, boosting both effect and raising money potential.

Manageability isn't simply a trendy expression for Rethinking Lavishness in Friendly Capabilities; it's an essential part of its occasion arranging ethos. The organization effectively incorporates eco-accommodating practices, from obtaining locally to carrying out squander decrease measures. The obligation to manageability isn't just a sign of approval for momentum natural worries; it mirrors a well established liability to the climate and a dream for a more supportable occasion industry.

Client fulfillment isn't only a measurement for Rethinking Excess in Friendly Capabilities; it's a demonstration of its obligation to greatness. The group moves toward each venture with a cooperative mentality, seeing clients not simply as supporters yet as accomplices in the innovative strategy. This cooperative soul encourages trust and straightforwardness, making an establishment for fruitful and persevering through connections. In an industry where notoriety is vital, Rethinking Luxury in Friendly Capabilities' devotion to surpassing assumptions has brought about a constant stream of gleaming tributes from fulfilled clients.

Advancement is the soul of Reclassifying Lavishness in Friendly Capabilities. The organization embraces arising advances to improve the general occasion insight. Virtual and cross breed occasions, expanded reality, and intelligent components are consistently woven into the texture of its contributions, making vivid and drawing in encounters that rise above the limits of traditional occasions.

Post-occasion assessments and criticism systems are fundamental to Rethinking Excess in Friendly Capabilities' obligation to ceaseless improvement. Gaining from every occasion isn't simply a training; a crucial standard guarantees each ensuing occasion expands upon the triumphs of its ancestors, increasing present expectations of greatness with each endeavor.

The cutthroat idea of the occasion business requires a ground breaking way to deal with business improvement. Reclassifying Lavishness in Friendly Capabilities effectively looks for new open doors for development and extension. Vital organizations, statistical surveying, and a proactive position towards industry patterns position the organization as a powerful player in a consistently developing scene.

Schooling and information sharing are basic mainstays of Rethinking Luxury in Friendly Capabilities' corporate culture. The group is devoted to remaining at the bleeding edge of the most recent patterns, advances, and best practices in the business. This responsibility reaches out past inside preparing projects to include outer drives like studios, online classes, and mentorship programs, adding to the general development and improvement of the occasion the executives local area.

The worldwide reach of Reclassifying Luxury in Friendly Capabilities verifies its capacity to rise above geological limits. The organization has effectively executed occasions on a worldwide scale, exploring different social scenes with artfulness.

This worldwide point of view expands the organization's customer base as well as enhances its innovative range, mixing a cosmopolitan energy into each occasion it embraces.

Social obligation is woven into the actual texture of Reclassifying Excess in Friendly Capabilities. Past making remarkable encounters, the organization effectively looks for ways of rewarding the local area. Whether through magnanimous occasions, associations with non-benefit associations, or drives that help nearby networks, Reclassifying Luxury in Friendly Capabilities endeavors to have a constructive outcome that stretches out a long ways past the domain of occasion the executives.

The future of Reclassifying Luxury in Friendly Capabilities is set apart by a proceeded with devotion to greatness and an unfaltering quest for development. The organization imagines itself as a member as well as a pioneer, forming the future scene of high-profile social capabilities. From spearheading patterns to rethinking the limits of excess, Reclassifying Lavishness in Friendly Capabilities tries to be a main thrust that sets new benchmarks for the business on a worldwide scale.

Chapter 8

The Business of Luxury

The matter of extravagance is a multi-layered and dynamic industry that traverses many areas, from style and assistants to vehicles and cordiality. At its center, the extravagance business rotates around the creation and conveyance of top of the line, elite items and encounters that take care of an insightful and well-off customers.

One of the central attributes of the extravagance business is its emphasis on craftsmanship and quality. Extravagance brands are frequently connected with careful meticulousness, utilizing the best materials and utilizing gifted craftsmans to make items that are tastefully satisfying as well as solid. This obligation to quality is a vital differentiator for extravagance brands, separating them from mass-market partners.

In the domain of design, extravagance houses have for some time been respected for their capacity to start precedents and characterize style. From notorious couture manifestations to prepared to-wear assortments, these brands influence their legacy and plan ability to set up a good foundation for themselves as referees of taste. The charm of selectiveness assumes a urgent part in the outcome of extravagance design, as customers look to separate themselves through one of a kind and restricted release pieces.

Past design, the extravagance business expands its impact into the universe of embellishments. Very good quality watches, gems, and purses are desired things that act as superficial points of interest for the individuals who can manage the cost of them. The craftsmanship and plan of these embellishments frequently mirror the legacy and mastery of the brands behind them, adding to their allure as ageless speculations.

Lately, the extravagance auto area has seen a shift towards customization and personalization. Extravagance vehicle makers presently offer customized choices, permitting clients to fit each part of their vehicles to suit their inclinations. This pattern highlights the developing longing for exceptional and customized encounters inside the extravagance market.

The idea of extravagance additionally stretches out into the domain of movement and neighborliness. Elite retreats, confidential islands, and extravagance travels take special care of people looking for lavish encounters and unmatched assistance. The interest for custom travel encounters has led to a specialty inside the extravagance business, where knowing voyagers will pay a premium for tailor-made undertakings.

The matter of extravagance isn't just about items and encounters yet in addition about narrating. Extravagance marks frequently weave stories around their legacy, craftsmanship, and values to make a feeling of genuineness and association with shoppers. This narrating goes past conventional promoting; it turns into a basic piece of the brand's personality, forming the way in which shoppers see and connect with the items or administrations advertised.

The ascent of advanced stages has altogether affected the extravagance business, modifying the manner in which brands cooperate with shoppers. Web-based entertainment, specifically, has turned into an integral asset for extravagance brands to exhibit their items, draw in with crowds, and construct a local area of steadfast clients. Nonetheless, this shift to computerized channels likewise presents difficulties, as keeping up with restrictiveness in a computerized age requires a sensitive equilibrium.

Web based business has arisen as a huge channel for extravagance deals, permitting brands to contact worldwide crowds and smooth out the buying system. Be that as it may, the web-based scene achieves concerns fake items and weakening of brand picture. Extravagance brands should cautiously explore the advanced space, executing hearty confirmation gauges and developing an internet based presence that lines up with the brand's qualities.

The Chinese market has turned into a urgent player in the extravagance business, with a developing number of princely buyers driving interest for top of the line items. Extravagance brands are decisively growing their presence in China, laying out leader stores and fashioning organizations with neighborhood powerhouses. Understanding the remarkable inclinations and social subtleties of the Chinese customer has become fundamental for progress in the worldwide extravagance market.

Supportability has likewise arisen as a basic thought for the extravagance business. As buyers become all the more ecologically cognizant, extravagance brands are feeling the squeeze to embrace manageable practices in their creation cycles and supply chains. The shift towards moral and eco-accommodating practices mirrors a more extensive cultural pattern towards mindful utilization, testing conventional thoughts of overabundance inside the extravagance business.

The resale market has encountered critical development inside the extravagance area, energized by a longing for manageability and moderateness. Used extravagance things, from style parts of very good quality watches, are tracking down another life through internet based resale stages. Extravagance brands are starting to recognize and try and embrace the resale market, perceiving its capability to expand the lifecycle of their items and contact a more extensive crowd.

The connection among innovation and extravagance is advancing, with developments like expanded reality (AR) and computer generated reality (VR) being integrated into the shopping experience. Extravagance brands are investigating vivid innovations to make virtual display areas, permitting clients to encounter items in a computerized space. This assembly of innovation and extravagance presents new open doors for commitment and narrating.

The administration of brand picture is a pivotal part of the extravagance business. A cautiously organized picture draws in clients as well as impacts impression of eliteness and glory. Brand coordinated efforts with craftsmen, fashioners, and VIPs are normal procedures utilized by extravagance brands to improve their allure and contact new crowds. In any case, keeping up with command over the brand picture turns out to be seriously difficult in the time of virtual entertainment, where public discernment can be formed by viral patterns and client created content.

The idea of agelessness is profoundly imbued in the extravagance business. Dissimilar to quick mold or pattern driven ventures, extravagance marks frequently seek to make items that endure for an extremely long period. This accentuation on life span adds to the persevering through allure of extravagance merchandise, as shoppers view them as assets as well as speculations with an enduring heritage.

The worldwide idea of the extravagance business requires a comprehension of different societies and purchaser inclinations. Extravagance brands should tailor their techniques to reverberate with neighborhood tastes while keeping a firm worldwide character. This sensitive equilibrium requires a nuanced approach, as what reverberates in one market may not be guaranteed to mean outcome in another.

The job of forces to be reckoned with and brand diplomats has become progressively critical in the extravagance business. Coordinated efforts with compelling people furnish brands with a stage to contact new crowds and support their picture. Notwithstanding, the choice of brand envoys requires cautious thought, as lining up with some unacceptable characters can have negative repercussions on a brand's standing.

Chasing after development, some extravagance brands are embracing the idea of "see currently, purchase presently," upsetting the customary style schedule. This approach permits shoppers to buy things following they are displayed on the runway, disposing of the conventional delay between design shows and item accessibility. While this technique lines up with the moment delight mentality of the advanced age, it additionally challenges the selectiveness related with hanging tight for desired pieces.

The advancement of the extravagance business is interlaced with cultural changes and moving purchaser values. As more youthful ages grow up, their assumptions and inclinations apply effect on the business. Twenty to thirty year olds and Age Z, specifically, are driving interest for encounters over material belongings, pushing extravagance brands to reexamine their techniques and contributions.

The mission for genuineness has turned into a main thrust in the extravagance business. Purchasers are progressively attracted to brands that show straightforwardness, moral practices, and a certifiable obligation to social obligation. Extravagance brands are answering by incorporating manageability into their fundamental beliefs and conveying these drives to buyers who are effectively looking for items with a positive effect.

The idea of eliteness, a foundation of the extravagance business, is going through a change. While conventional ideas of restrictiveness were established in restricted admittance and excessive cost focuses, present day extravagance is likewise characterized by inclusivity and availability. Extravagance brands are embracing a more just methodology, utilizing computerized stages to draw in with a more extensive crowd and proposition section level items that act as entryways to the brand's universe.

The changing scene of retail has incited extravagance brands to reexamine their physical systems. Lead stores are at this point not simply places to sell items; they are vivid spaces that typify the brand's personality and ethos. Innovation is incorporated into the actual retail insight, obscuring the lines among on the web and disconnected shopping. The objective is to make a consistent and vital excursion for the client, from revelation to buy.

All in all, the matter of extravagance is a complex and steadily developing scene that envelops different areas and impacts. From design and assistants to auto and friendliness, the extravagance business is portrayed by a guarantee to craftsmanship, quality, and narrating. The ascent of computerized stages, the impact of the Chinese market, the significance of supportability, and the effect of innovation are forming the direction of the extravagance business.

As extravagance brands explore these difficulties and potential open doors, the immortal standards of restrictiveness, genuineness, and brand picture stay at the front. The convergence of custom and development characterizes the quintessence of extravagance.

8.1 The Economics Behind Five-Star Excellence

The financial matters behind five-star greatness in the cordiality business dig into a mind boggling trap of variables that add to the creation and upkeep of extravagance foundations. From store lodgings to fabulous hotels, the quest for five-star status includes fastidious meticulousness, a promise to excellent help, and an essential comprehension of monetary elements.

At the core of the financial matters of extravagance friendliness is the idea of interest and supply. Lavish lodgings position themselves at the more elite classes of the market, focusing on an insightful customer base able to pay a premium for a prevalent encounter. The interest for five-star facilities is driven by a mix of elements, including discretionary cashflow, way of life decisions, and the longing for eliteness. As economies flourish and people look for raised encounters, the interest for extravagance friendliness rises, making a rewarding business sector for top of the line foundations.

The inventory side of the situation includes the development, activity, and the board of lavish lodgings. Fabricating and keeping a five-star property requires significant venture, both with regards to capital consumption for development and continuous functional expenses. The engineering, inside plan, and conveniences of a lavish lodging are cautiously organized to summon a feeling of plushness and complexity. From resplendent halls to fastidiously planned suites, each component is made to add to the general climate of extravagance.

The area of a lavish lodging is a basic consider its financial achievement. Ideal places, for example, grand waterfronts, downtown areas, or restrictive retreat objections, add to the charm of the property and legitimize premium valuing. The financial feasibility of a lavish inn is frequently entwined with its capacity to offer an extraordinary and pleasant setting that improves the general visitor experience.

Functional costs assume a huge part in the financial matters of extravagance neighborliness. Staffing levels in five-star foundations are commonly higher than in lower-level lodgings, with an accentuation on profoundly prepared faculty equipped for conveying excellent assistance. The enlistment, preparing, and maintenance of talented staff add to the general expense construction of lavish lodgings. The wages and advantages gave to representatives mirror the obligation to conveying a prevalent visitor experience, however they likewise influence the main concern.

The meticulousness in lavish lodgings reaches out to the nature of materials utilized in development and inside plan. Fine decorations, premium cloths, and best in class innovation add to the general mood of extravagance and add to the expense of making and keeping up with these very good quality foundations. The financial matters of extravagance friendliness direct an eagerness to put resources into top-level materials that line up with the brand's picture and guidelines.

Promoting and marking are basic parts of the monetary methodology for lavish lodgings. Laying out and keeping serious areas of strength for a presence is essential for drawing in the objective market and legitimizing premium valuing. Showcasing endeavors frequently incorporate coordinated efforts with high-profile powerhouses, support in elite occasions, and the formation of outwardly staggering limited time materials. The objective is to situate the lodging as an image of glory and complexity, captivating knowing explorers to pick it over contenders.

The idea of restrictiveness is a foundation of the financial matters of extravagance neighborliness. Restricted room stock, confidential admittance to conveniences, and customized administrations add to the impression of selectiveness that is inseparable from five-star foundations. This selectiveness legitimizes more exorbitant costs as well as encourages a feeling of honor and notoriety among visitors, making an alluring and optimistic picture for the brand.

In the domain of extravagance accommodation, client experience is vital. The financial matters behind five-star greatness perceive that remarkable help isn't just an upper hand yet additionally an essential for progress. Lavish lodgings put resources into broad preparation programs for their staff, underscoring customized administration, scrupulousness, and the capacity to expect and surpass visitor assumptions. The financial matters of client experience in extravagance cordiality are reflected in the recurrent business and positive verbal exchange references that come about because of conveying a noteworthy stay.

Innovation assumes a double part in the financial matters of extravagance cordiality. On one hand, the combination of state of the art innovation improves the visitor experience, offering accommodation and personalization. From savvy room controls to consistent booking stages, innovation adds to the general appeal of lavish lodgings. Then again, the forthright venture and progressing upkeep of innovation foundation add to the functional expenses for these foundations. Finding some kind of harmony among development and cost productivity is a vital thought for lavish lodgings.

The worldwide idea of the extravagance cordiality industry presents extra financial variables. Worldwide travel patterns, international occasions, and monetary vacillations influence the progression of visitors to lavish lodgings. The capacity to adjust to changing economic situations, appeal to assorted social inclinations, and keep a reliable norm of greatness across various areas is a test that lavish lodging networks should explore. The financial matters of worldwide extravagance friendliness include a sensitive harmony among normalization and restriction to guarantee a strong brand personality while taking care of territorial subtleties.

Maintainability has arisen as a critical thought in the financial matters of extravagance cordiality. As natural awareness develops among shoppers, lavish inns are feeling the squeeze to embrace eco-accommodating practices. The execution of practical drives, from energy-productive innovations to squander decrease programs, lines up with worldwide natural objectives as well as takes care of the inclinations of an undeniably eco-cognizant customer base. The financial aspects of manageability in extravagance accommodation include forthright interests in green advancements, yet they can likewise bring about long haul cost reserve funds and positive brand discernment.

Income the board is a vital part of the financial matters of extravagance neighborliness. Estimating techniques, bundle contributions, and the administration of room stock assume a focal part in enhancing income for five-star foundations. Dynamic valuing models, which change room rates in light of interest, occasional varieties, and unique occasions, permit lavish lodgings to boost income during top periods while offering advancements to draw in visitors during more slow times. The capacity to offset premium estimating with key advancements is an expertise that adds to the monetary outcome of lavish lodgings.

The elements of the extravagance accommodation industry are additionally affected by changing buyer inclinations. The ascent of experiential travel, the interest for health contributions, and the longing for credible and vivid encounters are molding the development of lavish inns. Monetary contemplations in this setting include adjusting to these evolving inclinations, putting resources into new conveniences and administrations, and remaining in front of industry patterns to keep up with pertinence and seriousness.

The effect of outside occasions, for example, worldwide wellbeing emergencies or catastrophic events, adds a component of unusualness to the financial matters of extravagance neighborliness. The strength of lavish lodgings even with unexpected moves is a demonstration of their capacity to adjust and enhance. Emergency the executives, possibility arranging, and the capacity to console and hold client certainty are basic parts of the financial procedure for lavish lodgings confronting outer interruptions.

All in all, the financial matters behind five-star greatness in the cordiality business are an unpredictable transaction of interest and supply, functional expenses, marking and showcasing, client experience, innovation, worldwide contemplations, supportability, and income the executives. Lavish lodgings explore a perplexing scene where the quest for greatness includes significant interests in both unmistakable and immaterial components. The outcome of a lavish lodging isn't exclusively estimated by monetary measurements yet in addition by its capacity to convey an excellent encounter that legitimizes the exceptional paid by knowing visitors. As the elements of the extravagance accommodation industry keep on advancing, the monetary methodologies utilized by five-star foundations will shape the eventual fate of this selective and optimistic area.

8.2 Marketing Strategies for High-End Hospitality

Showcasing procedures for top of the line neighborliness are a nuanced mix of complexity, restrictiveness, and a profound comprehension of the ideal interest group. In the domain of lavish lodgings, resorts, and other premium facilities, a lot is on the line, and the opposition is furious. Making a promoting approach that reverberates with rich explorers, conveys the remarkable incentive, and keeps a quality of eliteness is urgent for outcome in the top of the line cordiality area.

At the center of promoting for very good quality cordiality is the idea of brand situating. Laying out an unmistakable and convincing brand character is the establishment whereupon all showcasing endeavors are constructed. This personality includes the actual characteristics of the property as well as the immaterial components, for example, the visitor experience, administration reasoning, and by and large mood. The brand situating fills in as a compass, directing each part of the showcasing system to guarantee consistency and reverberation with the ideal customer base.

The visual personality of a very good quality friendliness brand assumes a crucial part in conveying extravagance and refinement. From the logo and variety range to the plan of special materials, each visual component should mirror the class and refinement related with the brand. Excellent photography and videography are fundamental apparatuses for displaying the magnificence of the property, its conveniences, and the unmatched encounters it offers. The visual language turns into a strong vehicle for bringing out feelings and goals, making a longing among likely visitors to be essential for the extravagance story.

Advanced stages have become vital to the showcasing techniques of very good quality friendliness brands. The authority site fills in as the computerized retail facade, giving a virtual look into the universe of extravagance presented by the property. It isn't only an educational device yet a key touchpoint in the visitor's excursion, from the underlying revelation stage to booking and then some. The web architecture should reflect the brand's stylish, offer consistent route, and give far reaching data about facilities, conveniences, and restrictive contributions.

Website streamlining (Search engine optimization) is a basic part of computerized showcasing for very good quality cordiality. Guaranteeing that the property's site positions high in applicable list items is fundamental for drawing in natural rush hour gridlock. This includes improving site satisfied with significant watchwords, making excellent backlinks, and carrying out specialized Web optimization procedures. The objective is to situate the property as a top decision when wealthy explorers look for extravagance facilities, subsequently expanding perceivability and driving qualified traffic to the site.

Online entertainment stages assume a double part in the promoting blend for very good quality friendliness. They act as channels for exhibiting the optimistic way of life related with the property and as instruments for drawing in with the interest group. Visual-driven stages, for example, Instagram and Pinterest are especially compelling for sharing enamoring symbolism that conveys the embodiment of extravagance. Virtual entertainment promoting includes natural substance creation as well as essential publicizing efforts that target explicit socioeconomics and interests lined up with the brand.

Force to be reckoned with organizations have turned into a conspicuous element in the showcasing systems of very good quality friendliness brands. Teaming up with powerhouses who line up with the brand's qualities and take special care of the ideal crowd considers the making of real and optimistic substance.

Powerhouses carry an individual touch to the promoting story, sharing their encounters and making a feeling of association with their devotees. From go bloggers to way of life powerhouses, the right organizations can altogether intensify the span and effect of the brand's message.

Email promoting stays an intense instrument for top of the line neighborliness, offering an immediate and customized channel of correspondence with past and possible visitors. Constructing and portioning an email list considers designated informing in view of visitor inclinations, past collaborations, and booking history. Email missions can incorporate select offers, customized suggestions, and updates on forthcoming occasions or redesigns. The objective is to cultivate a feeling of steadfastness and keep the property top-of-mind for future itinerary items.

Key associations with extravagance travel services, visit administrators, and attendant services are basic to the showcasing environment of top of the line friendliness. Working together with these elements extends the span of the brand among wealthy voyagers who depend on organized encounters and customized administration. Favored organizations frequently bring about select advancements, added conveniences, and improved perceivability inside the organization of extravagance travel experts.

Occasions and encounters assume a key part in the showcasing methodologies for very good quality friendliness. Facilitating elite occasions, whether they are excellent openings, themed gatherings, or cozy social events, sets out open doors to grandstand the property to a select crowd. These occasions create buzz, draw in media inclusion, and give a stage to verbal exchange showcasing among persuasive participants. Arranged encounters, for example, spa withdraws, culinary occasions, or experience bundles, add to the property's story of extravagance and eliteness.

Advertising (PR) is a foundation of showcasing for top of the line neighborliness, utilizing media inclusion to construct validity and upgrade brand perceivability. Getting highlights in esteemed distributions, tourism publications, and way of life web journals helps position the property as an objective of decision for knowing voyagers. The specialty of narrating turns into a useful asset in PR, permitting the property to share its novel history, plan reasoning, and obligation to remarkable help.

Content advertising is a fundamental part of the general promoting methodology for top of the line accommodation. Making connecting with and enlightening substance upgrades the brand's web-based presence as well as positions it as an expert in the extravagance travel space. Blog entries, articles, and sight and sound substance can cover a scope of subjects, from objective advisers for in the background checks the property out. Content showcasing teaches, rouse, and interface with the crowd on a more profound level.

Personalization is a vital pattern in the showcasing techniques for very good quality cordiality. Prosperous explorers look for tailor made encounters that take special care of their singular inclinations and wants. From customized welcome conveniences to organized schedules, the capacity to expect and satisfy the remarkable necessities of every visitor adds to the property's standing for unmatched assistance. Personalization stretches out to showcasing correspondences, where designated messages and offers resound with the particular interests of various visitor portions.

Notoriety the board is a basic part of promoting for very good quality friendliness. Online surveys and appraisals on stages like TripAdvisor, Google, and Howl convey critical load in the dynamic course of prosperous voyagers. A proactive way to deal with overseeing and answering surveys, combined with a pledge to tending to visitor criticism, adds to a positive web-based standing. Positive audits act as supports of the property's greatness, affecting likely visitors in their dynamic cycle.

The idea of steadfastness programs has developed with regards to top of the line neighborliness. While conventional reliability programs in light of focuses and limits may not line up with the eliteness of extravagance brands, making customized dedication drives can cultivate rehash business. Customized advantages, selective admittance to occasions, and unique conveniences for rehash visitors add to a feeling of appreciation and acknowledgment. Devotion programs become a method for building long haul associations with visitors who appreciate and search out the brand's obligation to greatness.

Emergency the executives is a vital part of advertising for very good quality friendliness. Unanticipated occasions, from cataclysmic events to worldwide wellbeing emergencies, can affect the movement business and the view of explicit objections. Having a powerful emergency correspondence plan set up permits the property to answer quickly and straightforwardly, consoling visitors and keeping up with trust in the brand. Emergency the board includes alleviating quick difficulties as well as decisively remaking trust and situating the property for future achievement.

Measurements and examination are fundamental apparatuses for evaluating the viability of promoting systems in top of the line neighborliness. Following key execution pointers (KPIs, for example, site traffic, change rates, virtual entertainment commitment, and profit from speculation (return for capital invested) gives experiences into the effect of different showcasing drives. Dissecting visitor socioeconomics and booking designs considers an information driven way to deal with refining and improving the promoting methodology over the long haul.

All in all, showcasing techniques for top of the line cordiality are a dynamic and multi-layered try that includes a sensitive equilibrium of brand situating, computerized presence, powerhouse joint efforts, key organizations, occasions, advertising, content creation, personalization, notoriety the board, dependability drives, emergency the executives, and information driven

examination. The progress of an extravagance property in a cutthroat market depends on its capacity to make a convincing story that reverberates with princely explorers, lifts the visitor experience, and keeps an emanation of selectiveness. As the scene of extravagance travel develops, the techniques utilized by very good quality neighborliness brands will keep on adjusting, advance, and rethink the norms of greatness chasing drawing in and pleasing knowing visitors.

8.3 Navigating Challenges in Luxury Management

Exploring difficulties in extravagance the board requires a nuanced comprehension of the special elements and intricacies intrinsic in the very good quality area. Whether in design, cordiality, car, or some other extravagance space, the administration of extravagance brands requests an essential methodology that tends to issues going from moving buyer inclinations to financial vulnerabilities and the effect of innovation.

One of the chief difficulties in extravagance the executives is the developing idea of customer conduct. Prosperous purchasers, especially those having a place with more youthful ages, are progressively focusing on encounters over material belongings. This shift represents a test to customary extravagance marks that have long depended on the charm of restrictive items as superficial points of interest. Extravagance the board should adjust by offering experiential components, customized administrations, and a feeling of legitimacy to take special care of the changing inclinations of knowing purchasers.

The ascent of digitalization presents the two potential open doors and difficulties for extravagance the board. While computerized stages give a worldwide reach and an immediate line of correspondence with shoppers, they likewise represent a danger to the restrictiveness customarily connected with extravagance. The test lies in utilizing computerized devices without weakening the brand's renown. Extravagance the executives should cautiously organize online presence, taking part in refined advanced advertising while at the same time keeping a quality of selectiveness that lines up with the brand's character.

Duplicating and the multiplication of phony extravagance merchandise represent a huge test in the extravagance the board scene. As innovation propels, forgers become more skilled at recreating very good quality items, prompting potential income misfortunes and harm to mark notoriety. Viable enemy of duplicating measures, like imaginative bundling, validation advancements, and legitimate activities against forgers, are vital for extravagance the board to safeguard the brand and keep up with the apparent worth of certifiable items.

The globalization of extravagance markets presents intricacies for extravagance the board. Adjusting to assorted social subtleties, purchaser ways of behaving, and market patterns is fundamental for outcome in various districts.

Extravagance the board should find some kind of harmony between keeping a predictable brand picture internationally and taking care of the exceptional inclinations of neighborhood markets. This includes grasping social awarenesses, fitting showcasing techniques, and once in a while tweaking item contributions to resound with explicit districts.

Maintainability has arisen as a basic worry in the extravagance the board scene. As ecological mindfulness develops, purchasers progressively expect extravagance brands to take on maintainable practices. The test for extravagance the executives is to incorporate eco-accommodating drives without compromising the view of lavishness and craftsmanship. Offsetting maintainability with the customary ideas of overabundance and guilty pleasure is a sensitive undertaking that requires cautious thought and correspondence to the interest group.

The administration of HR is one more test in extravagance the board. Offering first class support and keeping up with the best expectations require a talented and committed labor force. Drawing in, preparing, and holding ability that lines up with the brand's ethos and values is a nonstop test. Extravagance the board should put resources into representative turn of events, make a positive work environment culture, and guarantee that staff individuals epitomize the brand's obligation to greatness in each cooperation with clients.

Monetary vulnerabilities, including worldwide monetary slumps and international unsteadiness, present difficulties for extravagance the executives. The extravagance area is delicate to changes in customer certainty and spending designs. Extravagance the board should be deft in answering financial difficulties, changing valuing procedures, and broadening contributions to explore times of vulnerability. Making a strong plan of action that can endure monetary vacillations is a critical part of viable extravagance the board.

The job of powerhouses and brand representatives presents the two potential open doors and difficulties for extravagance the board. Working together with compelling people can essentially intensify a brand's compass and effect. In any case, the test lies in choosing ministers who line up with the brand's qualities and keeping up with command over the account. Stumbles in force to be reckoned with associations can prompt brand weakening or harm, stressing the significance of fastidious screening and vital coordinated efforts in extravagance the board.

Safeguarding licensed innovation is a vital worry for extravagance the board. From famous plans to mark logos, the protected innovation of extravagance brands is an important resource that requires cautious shielding. The test lies in forestalling unapproved use, impersonation, and falsifying. Extravagance the executives should carry out strong lawful techniques, participate in proactive observing, and make a quick move against encroachments to safeguard the brand's novel character and imaginative resources.

Keeping up with restrictiveness is a continuous test in extravagance the executives. As the idea of extravagance develops, keeping a feeling of extraordinariness and restrictiveness turns out to be more mind boggling. Restricted version discharges, custom administrations, and cautiously organized coordinated efforts are systems utilized by extravagance the board to make an impression of restrictiveness. Nonetheless, finding some kind of harmony among selectiveness and availability is essential to guarantee that the brand remains optimistic without distancing possible clients.

The elements of retail are going through a change, introducing difficulties for extravagance the executives. The shift to internet shopping and the ascent of web based business have upset conventional retail models. Extravagance the board should adjust by making consistent omnichannel encounters that coordinate on the web and disconnected channels. The test lies in protecting the customized and vivid parts of extravagance shopping while at the same time utilizing the accommodation and openness presented by advanced stages.

Emergency the executives is difficult for extravagance the board. Unanticipated occasions, from item reviews to advertising emergencies, can significantly affect an extravagance brand's standing. Extravagance the executives should be ready to answer quickly, straightforwardly, and successfully to moderate the harm and modify trust. The capacity to explore emergencies while maintaining the brand's qualities and picture is a demonstration of the strength of extravagance the executives.

The job of imaginativeness and craftsmanship is integral to the character of numerous extravagance brands, introducing a remarkable test for extravagance the board. Adjusting the requests of large scale manufacturing with the obligation to high quality greatness requires key navigation. Extravagance the executives should guarantee that creation processes satisfy the most elevated guidelines while fulfilling market needs. The test lies in keeping up with the respectability of craftsmanship despite adaptability and business pressures.

Production network the board presents difficulties for extravagance the executives, especially in guaranteeing the obtaining of the best materials and keeping up with moral practices. From outlandish calfskins to uncommon gemstones, the validness and moral starting points of materials are basic for extravagance brands. Extravagance the executives should lay out straightforward and mindful inventory chains to address buyer worries about manageability and moral obtaining.

Adjusting to the changing socioeconomics of extravagance purchasers is really difficult for extravagance the executives. The inclinations and upsides of more youthful ages, like Recent college grads and Age Z, vary from those of conventional extravagance buyers.

Extravagance the executives should comprehend and answer the developing assumptions for these socioeconomics, from an attention on encounters to an accentuation on friendly obligation. Interfacing with more youthful customers while holding the dedication of existing customer base requires a nuanced approach in extravagance the executives.

Innovation interruption presents difficulties and open doors for extravagance the executives. The joining of advancements like computerized reasoning, expanded reality, and augmented reality into the extravagance experience improves personalization and commitment. Nonetheless, the test lies in embracing development without compromising the immortal allure of extravagance. Extravagance the executives should cautiously incorporate innovation to improve as opposed to eclipse the human touch and craftsmanship related with top of the line brands.

The idea of immortality is a test and a main quality for extravagance the executives. While patterns travel every which way, extravagance brands seek to make items and encounters that go the distance. The test lies in adjusting the quest for development with the protection of legacy and custom. Extravagance the board should explore the pressure between remaining significant in a unique market and maintaining the immortal charm that characterizes the substance of extravagance.

All in all, exploring difficulties in extravagance the executives requires a comprehensive and versatile methodology that tends to the diverse elements of the top of the line area. From moving shopper inclinations to the effect of innovation, monetary vulnerabilities, and the journey for maintainability, extravagance the board should be light-footed, vital, and focused on maintaining the qualities and personality of the brand. As the extravagance scene advances, the difficulties and potential open doors looked by extravagance the executives will keep on forming the business, affecting how top of the line brands draw in with their crowds and keep up with their situation as images of complexity, eliteness, and persevering through greatness.

8.4 Trends and Forecasts in Luxury Travel

Patterns and gauges in extravagance travel offer a brief look into the developing inclinations, ways of behaving, and assumptions for well-to-do voyagers. As the movement business goes through fast changes impacted by worldwide occasions, mechanical progressions, and moving buyer values, extravagance travel is at the front line of development. Understanding the arising patterns and estimating future improvements is urgent for partners in the extravagance travel area, including lodgings, visit administrators, and specialist co-ops.

Personalization is a key pattern forming the scene of extravagance travel. Princely voyagers progressively look for custom and custom encounters that take care of their singular inclinations and wants. From customized schedules created to explicit interests to restrictive admittance to far-reaching developments, extravagance travel is getting away from one-size-fits-all bundles.

Personalization stretches out past the actual objective, enveloping each part of the excursion, from convenience decisions to arranged exercises, permitting voyagers to make genuinely remarkable and significant encounters.

Health and experiential travel keep on acquiring conspicuousness in extravagance travel patterns. Wellbeing cognizant shoppers are looking for movement encounters that give unwinding as well as add to their general prosperity. Extravagance resorts are consolidating spa withdraws, care programs, and vivid health exercises into their contributions. Experiential travel goes past customary touring, underscoring involved, valid experiences with neighborhood culture, nature, and cooking, mirroring a craving for significant and extraordinary excursions.

Manageability has turned into a focal concentration in extravagance travel patterns. Well-off explorers are progressively aware of their natural effect and look for movement encounters that line up with economical practices. Lavish lodgings and visit administrators are answering by executing eco-accommodating drives, like diminishing carbon impressions, limiting single-use plastics, and supporting neighborhood preservation endeavors. The interest for practical extravagance travel encounters mirrors a more extensive worldwide shift towards mindful and moral the travel industry.

Remote and more unfamiliar locations are acquiring prevalence in extravagance travel patterns. Prosperous explorers are looking for selective and outside of what might be expected areas, driven by a longing for protection, legitimacy, and a break from swarmed traveler areas of interest. Distant extravagance lodges, confidential island resorts, and custom wild encounters take care of the people who esteem disconnection and will wander past conventional travel objections looking for interesting and immaculate scenes.

Innovation is assuming an undeniably huge part in extravagance travel patterns, changing the manner in which voyagers plan and experience their excursions. Man-made brainpower (artificial intelligence) and AI are being used to improve personalization, giving custom-made proposals in view of individual inclinations and ways of behaving. Computer generated reality (VR) and expanded reality (AR) are being coordinated into the arranging system, permitting voyagers to investigate objections and facilities in vivid detail prior to simply deciding.

Contactless and touchless encounters have turned into a need in extravagance travel patterns, advanced rapidly by the worldwide wellbeing emergency. Voyagers presently anticipate negligible actual contact during their excursions, from contactless registrations at inns to touchless installment choices. Extravagance travel suppliers are putting resources into innovation that works with a consistent and clean travel insight, guaranteeing that security and prosperity stay central worries for well-to-do explorers.

The ascent of private travel choices is a remarkable pattern in extravagance travel. Personal luxury planes, sanctioned yachts, and selective estate rentals appeal to wealthy voyagers looking for upgraded protection, security, and command over their movement encounters. Confidential travel choices consider customized schedules, keeping away from swarmed air terminals, and guaranteeing a more elevated level of solace and selectiveness. Thus, extravagance travel is moving towards additional private and disconnected methods of transportation and convenience.

Culinary the travel industry has turned into a characterizing pattern in extravagance travel, with well-to-do explorers putting a top notch on uncommon feasting encounters. Food and drink assume an essential part in the general travel insight, with explorers looking for objections known for their culinary greatness. Lavish lodgings are teaming up with famous gourmet specialists, offering organized gastronomic encounters, and displaying nearby food to take care of the developing interest for culinary the travel industry among prosperous voyagers.

Multigenerational travel is a rising pattern in extravagance travel, mirroring the changing elements of family get-aways. Prosperous families are progressively picking encounters that take care of various age gatherings, guaranteeing that everybody, from grandparents to kids, partakes in the excursion. Extravagance resorts are adjusting by offering family-accommodating conveniences, kid-accommodating exercises, and far reaching convenience choices to oblige the different requirements and inclinations of multigenerational explorers.

Online entertainment impact keeps on forming extravagance travel patterns. Princely explorers are motivated by outwardly engaging objections, encounters, and facilities displayed via online entertainment stages. Instagram-commendable areas and the longing to impart selective encounters to a worldwide crowd impact travel choices. Extravagance travel suppliers are utilizing virtual entertainment powerhouses and developing areas of strength for a presence to interface with their interest group and feature the charm of their contributions.

Space the travel industry is arising as an optimistic pattern in extravagance travel. Albeit still in its beginning phases, space the travel industry is acquiring consideration among prosperous people who fantasy about wandering past Earth's climate. Confidential space travel organizations are investigating ways of offering suborbital and orbital encounters to those able to set out on a definitive extravagance experience. While the openness and practicality of room the travel industry are as of now restricted, it addresses a cutting edge pattern that catches the creative mind of the extravagance travel market.

Blockchain innovation is making advances into extravagance travel patterns, especially in resolving issues connected with security, straightforwardness, and trust. Blockchain's decentralized and secure nature is being investigated for applications in booking processes, dedication programs, and guaranteeing the legitimacy of extravagance travel encounters.

The utilization of blockchain can upgrade information insurance, smooth out exchanges, and give a certain record of the whole travel venture, adding to a safer and straightforward extravagance travel environment.

The idea of slow travel is getting momentum in extravagance travel patterns. Rather than speedy schedules, slow travel energizes an all the more comfortable and vivid investigation of objections. Well-to-do explorers are looking for long visits, permitting them to associate with nearby culture, enjoy novel encounters, and stay away from the pressure of hurried itineraries. Lavish lodgings are adjusting to this pattern by offering long-term visit bundles and empowering a more profound association with the objective.

Changing socioeconomics are affecting extravagance travel patterns, with the ascent of millennial and Age Z explorers forming the business' heading. More youthful ages focus on encounters, realness, and social obligation in their movement decisions. Extravagance travel suppliers are adjusting by making encounters that resound with the upsides of more youthful explorers, from reasonable drives to exceptional and Instagram-commendable exercises that take special care of the longing for shareable minutes.

Social drenching and instructive travel encounters are acquiring ubiquity in extravagance travel patterns. Wealthy explorers are looking for chances to draw in with neighborhood networks, partake in social trades, and gain experiences into the legacy and customs of objections. Lavish inns are teaming up with nearby craftsmans, offering social studios, and giving organized encounters that permit voyagers to develop how they might interpret the spots they visit, adding to a more significant and enhancing travel insight.

Foreseeing the eventual fate of extravagance travel includes thinking about more extensive worldwide patterns. The continuous effect of the Coronavirus pandemic, international movements, and financial improvements will without a doubt impact the direction of extravagance travel. Adaptability and flexibility will be key variables in extravagance travel patterns, as voyagers look for confirmation and choices despite vulnerabilities. Also, the business' capacity to adjust the developing interest for selectiveness with advancing purchaser assumptions will shape the future scene of extravagance travel.

All in all, patterns and conjectures in extravagance travel mirror a dynamic and developing scene impacted by moving customer inclinations, mechanical progressions, and worldwide occasions. From personalization and supportability to arising advancements and the ascent of experiential travel, the extravagance head out area keeps on adjusting to meet the longings and assumptions for rich voyagers. As the business explores the difficulties and open doors introduced by the changing travel scene, remaining receptive to these patterns is fundamental for extravagance make a trip suppliers looking to offer unmatched encounters and keep up with their situation at the cutting edge of the very good quality travel market.

Chapter 9

Beyond the Facade

In the core of the clamoring city, where transcending high rises penetrated the sky and the murmur of metropolitan life reverberated through the roads, there existed a world past the veneer. In the midst of the bedlam of the city, stowed away stories unfurled, and lives entwined in manners concealed by the rushed bystander.

The city's outside, a glimmering embroidery of steel and glass, introduced a deception of flawlessness. However, inside the disguised corners and in secret, an alternate reality arose — an embroidery woven with strings of battle, satisfaction, sadness, and versatility. Here the surface facade misrepresented the intricacy of human experience.

In the core of the monetary locale, where business head honchos made bargains that formed the destiny of enterprises, a café named "Congruity Brews" stood subtly. Its unpretentious exterior covered a microcosm of different stories. The smell of newly ground espresso beans floated through the air, blending with the murmurs of discussions that painted the material of the spot.

In the midst of the variety of benefactors nursing their cups of steaming espresso, Maria, an independent craftsman, tracked down comfort in her corner. Her exhausted sketchbook and some dark espresso were her colleagues as she drenched herself in the realm of her creative mind. By all accounts, she was simply one more face in the group, however her representations recounted accounts of dreams and yearnings, of a daily existence past the bounds of cultural assumptions.

As Maria outlined, a man named Victor, in a custom-made suit that discussed corporate achievement, found a spot at a close by table. His eyes, nonetheless, double-crossed an exhaustion that reflected the heaviness of his obligations. Past the veneer of thriving, Victor wrestled with the penances requested by his high-stakes profession. His family, ancient history in the persistent quest for progress, waited behind the scenes of his viewpoints like an unpleasant song.

Concordance Brews was in excess of a café; it was a sanctuary for spirits looking for shelter from the tumult of their day to day routines. The barista, Olivia, realized the regulars by name and grasped their implicit stories. Her inviting grin and certified interest changed the café into a local area — a space where associations were manufactured past the surface connections of a bustling world.

Somewhere else in the city, settled between transcending apartment buildings and corporate central command, was a recreational area that filled in as a desert garden of vegetation. The exterior of nature stood out forcefully from the encompassing metropolitan wilderness. In this peaceful setting, families accumulated, youngsters played, and old couples tracked down relief on endured seats.

In the midst of the giggling of youngsters playing tag and the stirring leaves above, Clara, a resigned teacher, went for her everyday walk. Her endured hands gripped a chain connected to Max, her devoted canine buddy. Clara's eyes, however matured, shone with an insight that exuded from a long period of encounters. She had seen the city advance, change, and now and again, disintegrate underneath the heaviness of progress.

As Clara strolled along the twisting ways of the recreation area, she experienced a youthful couple, Emily and David, sharing a sweeping under the shade of an old oak tree. Their chuckling reverberated through the air, blending with the tune of birds roosted on the tree's limbs. By all accounts, their adoration appeared to be a storybook sentiment, yet underneath the veneer, instabilities and fears had their influence.

Emily, a yearning author, wrestled with self-question that hid in the shadows of her imagination. David, a natural extremist, confronted the overwhelming errand of supporting for change in a world that frequently opposed it. Their adoration, certifiable and significant, wove a story of versatility against the background of a consistently impacting world.

The recreation area, with its mosaic of converging lives, turned into an embroidery of shared encounters. Unbeknownst to the relaxed onlooker, every individual conveyed a story that additional profundity to the aggregate story. The older man taking care of pigeons by the wellspring had once been a conflict veteran, and the youthful craftsman drawing the scene had as of late defeated an incapacitating sickness.

Past the veneer of the city's greatness, the human soul unfurled in heap ways. In the calmer areas, where the mood of life moved at a gentler speed, networks flourished, and people tracked down comfort in straightforwardness. One such area was Maplewood, where columns of curious houses lined the roads like pages in a storybook.

In one of these houses, carried on with a lady named Elena. Her nursery, a kaleidoscope of dynamic sprouts, mirrored her energy for supporting life. Past the veneer of schedule, Elena held onto confidential — the upper room, a mother lode of recollections epitomized in dusty photograph collections and endured diaries. Every curio held a part of her previous, a demonstration of the progression of time and the strength of the human soul.

Elena's neighbor, Mr. Johnson, a resigned teacher with a propensity for cosmology, spent his nights looking at the stars from his lawn. Past the veneer of his insightful disposition, lay a well established wonder for the universe — an oddity that rose above the limits old enough. His telescope, an entryway to far off systems, associated him to the immensity of the universe, offering a point of view past the bounds of natural worries.

Maplewood, with its tree-lined roads and public soul, remained as a demonstration of the magnificence of effortlessness. Neighbors knew one another by name, kids played together in the nearby park, and the smell of home-prepared feasts floated through the air during end of the week social affairs. Past the veneer of rural predictability, Maplewood exemplified the quintessence of an associated local area.

As day went to night, the city changed into an embroidery of lights, each gleam addressing a story ready to be told. The neon indications of amusement regions called, promising a universe of energy and redirection. Among the groups, people looked for shelter from the requests of the real world, submerging themselves in the lively nightlife that beat underneath the surface.

In a faintly lit jazz club named "Melodic Murmurs," the feel reverberated with the melancholic types of a saxophone. The supporters, a different gathering of evening people, tracked down comfort in the mood of the music. Among them was Sophia, a legal counselor by day, who shed the bounds of her corporate persona to lose herself in the improvisational songs that resounded with the back and forth movement of life.

Situated at the bar, Imprint, a disappointed writer, breast fed his beverage as he mulled over the condition of the world. Past the veneer of his indifferent outside, a fire for truth consumed inside him — a craving to disclose the secret stories that influenced society. The jazz club, with its faint lights and deep tunes, turned into a safe-haven for those looking for significance past the outer layer of their reality.

As the night unfurled, the city uncovered its double nature — the amazing exterior that charmed the world and the complex embroidered artwork of stories woven in the shadows. Every road, each structure, and each face conveyed a story that rose above the limits of appearances. The city, with its perpetual movement and dynamic energy, reflected the intricacy of the human experience.

In the core of the city, where the over a significant time span coincided, an architecturally significant area remained as a demonstration of the persevering through nature of time. Cobbled roads and extremely old structures murmured stories of a past time. The veneer of these designs bore the scars of time, and inside their walls, reverberations of the past resounded.

Amelia, a student of history enthusiastically for safeguarding legacy, committed her life to revealing the tales implanted in the blocks and mortar of the architecturally significant area. Past the exterior of compositional magnificence, she saw an obligation to shield the stories that molded the city's personality. In her mission, she coincidentally found neglected letters, curios, and untold mysteries that illustrated the city's advancement.

The architecturally significant area turned into a material where the layers of time interlaced, making a mosaic of stories that rose above ages. Guests meandered through the cobblestone roads, unmindful of the spirits of the past that waited in the air. The city, with its consistently evolving scene, clutched its set of experiences like a treasured legacy.

In the edges of the city, where nature and development converged, a local area ranch named "Verde Valley" flourished. Past the exterior of urbanization, this desert spring of plant life remained as a demonstration of maintainable living. Families kept an eye on their plots, developing natural vegetables and embracing a way of life that blended with the earth.

Among the occupants was Jake, a previous corporate leader who exchanged the substantial wilderness for the serenity of Verde Valley. His hands, once familiar with the dash of a console, presently tracked down comfort in the dirt. Past the veneer of progress, Jake found satisfaction in the effortlessness of a day to day existence associated with the land.

Verde Valley, with its collective soul and obligation to ecological stewardship, encapsulated a dream of an amicable conjunction among mankind and nature. The occupants, limited by a common obligation to maintainability, tracked down a safe-haven that rose above the restrictions of current living.

As the city throbbed with life, there existed pockets of quiet where people looked for shelter from the commotion of the world. The city's parks, libraries, and secret nooks became asylums for reflection and consideration. In these spaces, individuals stood up to their deepest contemplations, desires, and fears, revealing the intricacies that stayed underneath the surface.

In the terrific library that remained as a stronghold of information, Thomas, an older book nut, spent his days submerged in the composed word. Past the veneer of his delicacy, his psyche crossed immense scenes of writing, exploring the domains of fiction and reasoning. The library, with its transcending racks and quieted murmurs, turned into an entry to different universes — a shelter for those looking for break and edification.

At a reflection garden concealed inside the city's heart, Beauty, a youthful expert wrestling with the tensions of progress, looked for serenity in the cadenced progression of a close by wellspring. Past the veneer of her ready disposition, a conflict under the surface unfurled — a mission for balance and internal harmony in a world that ceaselessly requested more.

The city, with its different scenes and crossing lives, reflected the complicated embroidered artwork of the human experience. Past the exterior of its transcending structures and clamoring roads, stories unfurled — accounts of adoration, misfortune, win, and versatility. The city, in the entirety of its glory, turned into an impression of the aggregate excursion of the people who called it home.

In the shadow of the city's horizon, a destitute sanctuary named "Safe house of Trust" remained as a guide of sympathy. Past the exterior of honor that characterized the city's financial scene, an alternate reality existed for the individuals who explored the brutal landscape of vagrancy. Safe house of Trust, with its comfortable beds and hot feasts, gave a life saver to the people who had gotten lost in the noise of society.

Among the safe house's inhabitants was Sarah, a once-effective financial specialist whose life disentangled because of unexpected conditions. Past the veneer of her worn out garments and tired eyes, Sarah gripped to the desire for reconstructing her life. The haven, with its different local area of people confronting misfortune, turned into a demonstration of the versatility of the human soul.

Volunteers at Sanctuary of Trust, similar to James, a resigned nurture, committed their chance to offering a sympathetic hand to those out of luck. Past the veneer of the safe house's humble outside, a many-sided snare of help and compassion thrived. The city, with its differences and difficulties, wrestled with the juxtaposition of wealth and neediness, making a story of social intricacy.

As day break painted the sky in tints of pink and gold, the city mixed to life by and by. The morning rush reverberated through the roads, and the city's veneer sparkled in the early light. Inside the many-sided embroidered artwork of the city, people sought after their fantasies, stood up to their feelings of dread, and explored the maze of human association.

Past the veneer of standard, the city exemplified the embodiment of life's excursion — an excursion set apart by snapshots of win, snapshots of rout, and the consistent quest for significance. In the core of the city's tumult, where the ensemble of presence worked out in a bedlam of sounds and sights, every individual, each structure, and every story added profundity to the consistently developing story of the human experience.

Thus, the city remained as a demonstration of the versatility of the human soul, a material where the strokes of satisfaction and distress painted a work of art past the veneer. In the unending musicality of metropolitan life, the city uncovered its real essence — an impression of the multi-layered, interconnected, and perpetually captivating embroidery of presence.

9.1 Ethical Luxury

In a world driven by commercialization, where the quest for richness frequently comes at the expense of moral contemplations, the idea of moral extravagance arises as a contrast — a principled and reasonable way to deal with guilty pleasure. Past the appeal of lavishness, moral extravagance dives into the intricacies of creation, obtaining, and the effect of shopper decisions on both society and the climate.

At the core of moral extravagance lies a basic change in context — a takeoff from the customary mentality that likens extravagance with overabundance. All things being equal, moral extravagance embraces that genuine guilty pleasure includes the best materials and craftsmanship as well as a guarantee to social obligation and ecological stewardship.

In the domain of style, moral extravagance challenges the quick moving, expendable nature of the business. It advocates for straightforwardness in the production network, guaranteeing that each piece of clothing conveys a story liberated from double-dealing. Manageable materials, like natural cotton and reused textures, supplant their ordinary partners, decreasing the biological impression of style creation.

Consider a couture atelier where gifted craftsmans fastidiously make pieces of clothing with accuracy and care. Past the charm of the end result, the moral extravagance brand focuses on fair wages, safe working circumstances, and the protection of conventional craftsmanship. Each fasten turns into a demonstration of the human touch, and each creation recounts an account of moral polish.

The adornments business, frequently connected with the charm of uncommon gemstones and valuable metals, goes through a change in the domain of moral extravagance. Blood jewels and ecological corruption give approach to morally obtained diamonds and reused metals. Craftsmans, motivated by a guarantee to social and natural obligation, plan pieces that rise above temporary patterns, becoming immortal images of moral richness.

In the domain of gastronomy, moral extravagance reaches out to the table. A Michelin-featured café turns into a stronghold of feasible feasting, obtaining fixings locally and supporting ranchers who stick to moral rural practices. The culinary experience changes into a festival of cognizant extravagance, where each nibble recounts an account of capable cultivating, fair exchange, and culinary development.

The cordiality business, as well, embraces the ethos of moral extravagance. Five-star resorts flawlessly coordinate lavishness with supportability, utilizing eco-accommodating works on, limiting waste, and supporting nearby networks. The charm of a rich escape becomes interlaced with a promise to ecological protection, making an encounter that rises above the fleeting delight of extravagance.

Past material belongings, moral extravagance expands its impact into the domains of innovation and development. Hardware created with struggle free minerals and intended for life span rethink the connection among customers and devices. The charm of state of the art innovation blends with a promise to diminishing electronic waste and advancing moral work rehearses in the assembling system.

In the realm of expressive arts, moral extravagance challenges the thought of selectiveness. Exhibitions become spaces that hero variety, displaying craftsmen from underestimated networks and giving a stage to voices that have customarily been disregarded. Workmanship turns into a vehicle for social change, an impression of the moral qualities that support the idea of extravagance.

As buyers become more upright, the market answers with a multiplication of moral extravagance marks, each cutting its specialty in the scene of careful utilization. These brands perceive that extravagance isn't inseparable from overabundance yet can be a power for positive change. They focus on better standards without compromise, life span over superfluity, and the prosperity of both mankind and the planet.

The idea of moral extravagance isn't without its difficulties. Adjusting the quest for benefit with moral contemplations requires a fragile dance. The expense of practical materials and fair work might raise the sticker price, representing a boundary to openness. In any case, defenders of moral extravagance contend that this selectiveness can be an impetus for change, empowering purchasers to see extravagance as an interest in values as opposed to a temporary guilty pleasure.

Training assumes an essential part in the expansion of moral extravagance. As shoppers become more educated about the effect regarding their decisions, they employ their buying power as an instrument for change. The interest for straightforwardness and responsibility reshapes enterprises, convincing them to embrace moral practices and focus on supportability in light of an insightful buyer base.

Moral extravagance isn't simply a pattern however a change in perspective — a principal reconsideration of the connection among utilization and obligation. It challenges the thought that extravagance should come to the detriment of morals, welcoming a more nuanced comprehension of leading a sumptuous life.

In the corporate scene, moral extravagance rises above showcasing way of talking, appearing as a promise to corporate social obligation. Organizations perceive that their activities reach out past overall revenues, impacting the prosperity of networks and the wellbeing of the planet. Supportable practices, moral obtaining, and charitable drives become vital parts of an organization's character.

Consider a top of the line beauty care products brand that not just delivers savagery free and harmless to the ecosystem items yet additionally puts resources into drives that engage ladies in the networks where its fixings are obtained. The charm of the brand reaches out past the cosmetics range to envelop a story of strengthening, supportability, and moral magnificence principles.

The idea of moral extravagance crosses with the developing development toward moderation — a dismissal of overabundance for purposeful living. Moderation, frequently connected with an organized tasteful and an emphasis on fundamental belongings, adjusts consistently with the standards of moral extravagance. The accentuation on better standards no matter what, cognizant utilization, and a careful way to deal with material belongings resounds with people looking for a more significant association with their effects.

Chasing moral extravagance, joint efforts among brands and craftsmans become an amazing asset for positive change. Craftsmans, frequently from minimized networks, carry conventional craftsmanship to the very front, implanting extravagance items with social lavishness and validness. These joint efforts rise above simple monetary exchanges, cultivating connections based on common regard and shared values.

The ascent of moral extravagance corresponds with a developing consciousness of the ecological effect of the design business. Quick design, described by fast creation cycles and expendable articles of clothing, contributes altogether to contamination and waste. Moral extravagance disturbs this worldview, pushing for a shift toward slow style — a model that focuses on toughness, immortal plan, and moral creation rehearses.

In the realm of excellence and individual consideration, moral extravagance challenges the regular principles of magnificence. The business, frequently condemned for propagating unreasonable excellence standards, goes through a change toward inclusivity and legitimacy. Brands champion variety, including models of different ages, sizes, nationalities, and orientation characters. The appeal of excellence becomes entwined with the festival of uniqueness and self-articulation.

The idea of moral extravagance reaches out past individual utilization to impact the acts of whole ventures. Certificate norms, like Fair Exchange and B Corp, give a system to organizations to show their obligation to moral standards. These confirmations, perceived universally, offer customers a dependable method for recognizing items and administrations that line up with their qualities.

In the domain of engineering and inside plan, moral extravagance appears in maintainable structure rehearses and a pledge to natural obligation.

Originators focus on materials with low ecological effect, energy-proficient innovations, and an amicable joining with regular environmental elements. The charm of a lavish living space becomes indistinguishable from a commitment to environmental protection.

As the idea of moral extravagance gets forward momentum, it prompts a reconsideration of the actual meaning of extravagance. As of now not bound to a shallow quest for overabundance, extravagance becomes inseparable from an all encompassing and scrupulous lifestyle. The charm of moral extravagance lies in its capacity to reclassify superficial points of interest, supplanting obvious utilization with a more significant appreciation for the qualities that support plushness.

Pundits contend that the quest for moral extravagance stays an honor, open just to those with the monetary means to focus on values over reasonableness. The expense of maintainability, fair work, and moral obtaining might deliver moral extravagance blocked off to a huge part of the worldwide populace. Defenders recognize this test yet battle that the restrictiveness of moral extravagance can be an impetus for change, moving a change in shopper conduct and industry rehearses.

With regards to travel and relaxation, moral extravagance changes the manner in which people experience the world. Very good quality retreats embrace eco-accommodating works on, offering voyagers a chance to enjoy plushness while limiting their natural effect. Extravagance travel turns into a conductor for social trade, supporting nearby economies and cultivating a more profound comprehension of different networks.

The idea of moral extravagance isn't without its inconsistencies. The actual pith of extravagance frequently suggests a degree of overabundance or selectiveness, and the quest for moral standards might appear to be in conflict with these customary thoughts. Nonetheless, defenders contend that genuine extravagance lies in the arrangement of one's qualities with one's decisions — a pursuit that rises above realism and welcomes a more significant association with the world.

In the domain of money, moral extravagance stretches out to venture rehearses. Influence money management acquires unmistakable quality as people try to adjust their monetary portfolios to moral contemplations. Interests in reasonable undertakings, environmentally friendly power, and socially dependable drives become a method for people to use their abundance for positive change.

The style business, a noticeable player in the domain of extravagance, wrestles with the polarity between its customary models of utilization and the moral goal. Quick style, portrayed by fast creation cycles, minimal expense work, and dispensable articles of clothing, remains as an unmistakable difference to the standards of moral extravagance.

The charm of continually evolving patterns, energized by a culture of mass utilization, conflicts with the manageable practices pushed by the defenders of moral design.

The ascent of moral extravagance meets with the more extensive development toward cognizant commercialization — a change in outlook that focuses on the effect of buys on both the individual and the world at large. Shoppers, furnished with data about the social and ecological ramifications of their decisions, become influencers. The appeal of careful utilization lies in its capacity to change ordinary exchanges into significant demonstrations of obligation.

In the corporate domain, moral extravagance stretches out to the work environment, testing customary thoughts of accomplishment and representative prosperity. Organizations perceive that the charm of a satisfying workplace goes past monetary remuneration. Moral business rehearses, like fair wages, a guarantee to variety and incorporation, and an emphasis on representative prosperity, become necessary parts of an organization's personality.

The idea of moral extravagance prompts a reconsideration of promoting procedures. Realness turns into a foundation as brands endeavor to straightforwardly impart their moral qualities. The charm of an item or administration stretches out past its actual characteristics to include the story behind its creation, the qualities it addresses, and the positive effect it tries to make.

In the domain of innovation, moral extravagance challenges the regular direction of development. The charm of the most recent devices is tempered by a thought of the ecological and social outcomes of innovative advancement. Organizations, driven by moral objectives, focus on supportable practices in assembling, lessen electronic waste, and put resources into advancements that add to the improvement of society.

As moral extravagance picks up speed, it impacts the decisions in their regular daily existences. Customers, outfitted with an uplifted consciousness of the effect of their choices, look for items and administrations that line up with their qualities. The charm of moral utilization lies in its extraordinary potential — an aggregate change in conduct that resonates through enterprises, provoking a reconsideration of plans of action and cultural standards.

The idea of moral extravagance prompts a reexamination of generosity. The charm of giving rises above customary thoughts of noble cause, turning into a vital and purposeful demonstration of having a constructive outcome. Humanitarians, whether people or partnerships, adjust their providing for purposes that address foundational issues, advance supportability, and add to the prosperity of networks.

In the realm of training, moral extravagance stretches out to individuals decisions in chasing after information. The charm of esteemed foundations is reevaluated considering their obligation to moral practices, inclusivity, and social obligation.

Schooling turns into a channel for strengthening, cultivating an age of people who focus on values and moral contemplations in their quest for information.

The idea of moral extravagance highlights the interconnectedness of worldwide difficulties and the requirement for aggregate activity. Environmental change, social disparity, and moral contemplations underway are not secluded issues but rather interconnected features of a mind boggling framework. The charm of moral extravagance lies in its capability to add to a more comprehensive and supportable vision for what's in store.

In the domain of high end food, moral extravagance changes the gastronomic experience. The charm of Michelin-featured cafés reaches out past impeccable flavors and culinary development to include a promise to maintainable obtaining, fair work rehearses, and a festival of neighborhood fixings. Feasting turns into a multisensory venture that mirrors an upright way to deal with guilty pleasure.

As moral extravagance acquires conspicuousness, it challenges the actual substance of private enterprise and the customary models of monetary development. The appeal of unending development is reevaluated considering the limited assets of the planet. Feasible practices, round economies, and an emphasis on prosperity become necessary parts of a reconsidered financial worldview.

The ascent of moral extravagance meets with the more extensive development toward cognizant living — a comprehensive methodology that stretches out past individual decisions to include an aggregate liability regarding the prosperity of the planet and its occupants. The charm of cognizant living lies in its capability to rethink achievement, bliss, and the actual texture of human life.

All in all, moral extravagance addresses a change in perspective — a takeoff from the customary comprehension of richness as inseparable from overabundance. The charm of moral extravagance lies not in that frame of mind of assets but rather in the arrangement of one's qualities with one's decisions. It moves enterprises to focus on maintainability, fair work practices, and social obligation. The idea of moral extravagance welcomes people to reclassify achievement, joy, and the actual importance of an everyday routine very much experienced. As the world wrestles with the results of uncontrolled commercialization, moral extravagance arises as a guide — a pathway toward a more cognizant, manageable, and significant lifestyle.

9.2 Social Responsibility in High-End Hospitality

In the thin universe of top of the line cordiality, where extravagance and lavishness are the trademark, a developing accentuation on friendly obligation is reshaping the scene. Past the sparkling crystal fixtures and immaculate help, a reliable shift is happening — an acknowledgment that the charm of extravagance ought to be agreeably interlaced with a promise to cultural prosperity, natural stewardship, and moral strategic policies.

At the core of this change is a redefinition of extravagance itself. Generally connected with extravagance and eliteness, extravagance in very good quality neighborliness is presently developing to envelop a more extensive, more all encompassing point of view. The charm of plushness reaches out past rich facilities and Michelin-featured feasting to incorporate a certified obligation to having a beneficial outcome on the world.

One critical part of social obligation in very good quality accommodation is natural manageability. Lavish lodgings, settled in pleasant scenes or overshadowing metropolitan horizons, perceive the significance of limiting their environmental impression. The charm of an unblemished climate is protected through drives like energy-proficient practices, squander decrease, and the utilization of eco-accommodating materials in development and tasks.

Consider a top of the line resort arranged on the shores of a tropical heaven. The charm of its perfect sea shores and lavish environmental factors isn't only protected yet improved through a pledge to manageability. The retreat takes on sustainable power sources, carries out water protection gauges, and participates in reforestation endeavors to balance its effect. Extravagance, in this unique situation, turns into an overseer of the normal ponders that frequently act as the background for top of the line friendliness.

In the domain of eating, the idea of ranch to-table reaches out past a stylish culinary pattern to turn into a foundation of social obligation. Very good quality cafés, celebrated for their gastronomic greatness, develop associations with neighborhood ranchers and purveyors. The charm of a tasty dinner isn't separated from the excursion of the fixings — obtained morally, frequently naturally, and with a guarantee to supporting neighborhood networks.

In the cityscape, where lavish lodgings stand as compositional wonders, the test of dependable metropolitan improvement comes to the very front. The charm of an excellent inn isn't undermined by its obligation to limiting never-ending suburbia or adding to the rejuvenation of nearby areas. Top of the line friendliness turns into an impetus for positive change, guaranteeing that the financial advantages it carries are shared evenhandedly with the encompassing local area.

The obligation to social obligation in very good quality neighborliness stretches out to the core of activities — the labor force. The charm of rich facilities is supplemented by a devotion to fair work rehearses, representative prosperity, and the encouraging of a different and comprehensive work environment. Lavish inns become heroes of basic freedoms, esteeming their staff as representatives as well as indispensable supporters of the visitor experience.

In this worldview, the idea of social obligation reaches out past philanthropy to envelop an essential way to deal with local area commitment. Very good quality lodgings, perceptive of their effect on nearby economies, look to make a positive gradually expanding influence.

The charm of extravagance turns into a driver for work creation, abilities improvement, and the strengthening of networks that have these sanctuaries of richness.

Consider an extravagance resort arranged in a rustic region. The charm of disappearing to a detached heaven is supplemented by the retreat's obligation to drawing in with the neighborhood local area. Through organizations with neighborhood craftsmans, social trade projects, and interests in schooling and medical care, the retreat turns into a guide of capable the travel industry. Extravagance, in this specific situation, turns into a power for social upliftment.

The ascent of social obligation in very good quality neighborliness isn't just a reaction to changing customer assumptions; it is an affirmation of the business' interconnectedness with the more extensive structure holding the system together. Lavish lodgings perceive that their charm isn't separated from the difficulties and open doors introduced by the world at large. In this acknowledgment, they become problem solvers, utilizing their impact to improve the planet and its occupants.

As very good quality lodgings leave on their excursion of social obligation, the idea of capable extravagance travel becomes the overwhelming focus. The charm of investigating fascinating objections is flawlessly mixed with a promise to saving social legacy, regarding neighborhood customs, and limiting the ecological effect of movement. Extravagance voyagers become cognizant worldwide residents, looking for encounters that enhance their lives while contributing emphatically to the spots they visit.

In the domain of top of the line friendliness, social obligation stretches out to the actual texture of the visitor experience. The charm of customized administration and scrupulousness is supplemented by a pledge to moral obtaining, squander decrease, and the joining of feasible practices into each feature of a visitor's visit. Extravagance, in this specific circumstance, becomes inseparable from a reliable and vivid experience.

Think about a very good quality lodging that, as well as offering rich facilities, connects with visitors in maintainability drives. The charm of a lavish stay is uplifted by the chance for visitors to take part in neighborhood protection projects, support local area improvement drives, or add to ecological conservation. Extravagance, in this worldview, turns into a cooperative undertaking that rises above the customary limits among visitors and hosts.

The reconciliation of social obligation in top of the line cordiality isn't without its difficulties. Finding some kind of harmony among richness and moral contemplations requires a nuanced approach. The charm of restrictiveness, frequently connected with extravagance, might be seen as incongruent with the standards of inclusivity and openness that support dependable strategic policies. In any case, defenders contend that extravagance, when characterized by its positive effect on society and the climate, turns into a power for motivation and positive change.

In the domain of extravagance travel, the idea of voluntourism arises as a sign of social obligation. Very good quality inns curate encounters that permit visitors to contribute definitively to nearby networks while partaking in the charm of a rich escape. This type of mindful the travel industry goes past conventional cause, cultivating a more profound association among explorers and the objections they visit.

The charm of top of the line accommodation is many times intensified by the social lavishness of the locations where lavish lodgings are arranged. In perceiving this, the business progressively embraces a promise to social conservation and local area commitment. Lavish lodgings become benefactors of human expression, supporting neighborhood craftsmen and comprehensive developments. The charm of a lodging stay is raised by the chance for visitors to drench themselves in the energetic embroidery of the neighborhood culture.

In the time of virtual entertainment, the charm of very good quality neighborliness stretches out a long ways past the actual limits of a lodging. A property's obligation to social obligation turns into a piece of its image story, impacting the impression of expected visitors and the more extensive public. Lodgings that champion reasonable practices, local area commitment, and moral business become forerunners in a developing industry scene.

The reconciliation of social obligation in top of the line neighborliness additionally stretches out to the domain of innovation. The charm of state of the art developments, from savvy room controls to customized visitor encounters, is supplemented by a promise to diminishing the ecological effect of innovation. Lavish lodgings embrace energy-effective frameworks, put resources into eco-accommodating innovations, and carry out advanced arrangements that improve functional proficiency while limiting waste.

Consider a top of the line lodging that uses cutting edge innovation to follow and diminish its carbon impression. The charm of remaining in a mechanically progressed climate is enhanced by the information that the inn is effectively adding to ecological manageability. Extravagance, in this specific situation, turns into a combination of development and obligation.

The obligation to social obligation in top of the line neighborliness likewise appears in generous drives. Lavish lodgings perceive their job as supporters of the more extensive social texture and influence their assets to have a beneficial outcome. The charm of a top of the line lodging stretches out past its actual presence to incorporate its generous undertakings — whether supporting neighborhood good cause, subsidizing instructive projects, or adding to worldwide drives.

With regards to very good quality neighborliness, social obligation stretches out to emergency reaction and local area flexibility. Lavish lodgings, frequently arranged in regions inclined to catastrophic events or different emergencies, become anchors of help during testing times.

The appeal of these foundations isn't decreased by difficulty however is, as a matter of fact, improved by their obligation to quick and successful reactions that focus on the prosperity of visitors and nearby networks.

The ascent of social obligation in very good quality neighborliness prompts a reexamination of industry norms and confirmations. The charm of a renowned honor or confirmation is currently not exclusively founded on tasteful allure or visitor fulfillment yet additionally on a lodging's adherence to moral strategic policies, natural manageability, and local area commitment. Extravagance, in this developing scene, becomes inseparable from a pledge to greatness across various aspects.

9.3 Environmental Sustainability

In a time characterized by raising ecological worries, the basic for natural supportability has arisen as a core value across different spaces of human action. Past being a trendy expression, maintainability is an all encompassing methodology that perceives the reliance between human frameworks and the normal world. This change in outlook looks to fit financial, social, and ecological contemplations, guaranteeing that current activities don't think twice about capacity of people in the future to address their issues.

At the core of ecological maintainability lies a significant acknowledgment of the limited idea of Earth's assets. The charm of vast overflow, once inseparable from progress and success, is supplanted by a levelheaded affirmation that the planet works inside natural cutoff points. This change in context isn't an incrimination of progress however a require a more upright and adjusted way to deal with improvement.

The appeal of financial development, generally estimated by GDP (Gross domestic product), is reexamined inside the structure of supportability. Ecological maintainability challenges the predominant idea that limitless development is both attractive and achievable. All things considered, it advocates for a regenerative model that considers the limit of environments to help life and the requirement for impartial circulation of assets.

In the domain of horticulture, natural supportability rises above traditional works on, preparing for regenerative cultivating. The appeal of plentiful harvests is rethought inside the setting of soil wellbeing, biodiversity, and water preservation. Agroecological standards supplant synthetic concentrated approaches, underlining the cooperative connections between yields, domesticated animals, and the biological systems they possess.

Consider an economical ranch where permaculture standards guide development, and regenerative practices reestablish soil richness. The charm of this approach isn't exclusively in that frame of mind of harvests however in the subjective advantages — sound environments, upgraded versatility to environmental change, and a decreased biological impression.

Natural supportability in horticulture turns into a door to food security, biodiversity protection, and country thriving.

The idea of natural maintainability stretches out to metropolitan preparation, testing the charm of rambling urban areas portrayed by blockage and asset concentrated framework. Manageable metropolitan advancement embraces standards of smallness, green spaces, and effective public transportation. The charm of a lively cityscape is unpredictably woven with energy-proficient structures, squander decrease, and a promise to moderating the metropolitan intensity island impact.

In the structural domain, green structure rehearses become inseparable from natural supportability. The charm of inventive plans is combined with energy-effective innovations, inexhaustible materials, and an emphasis on limiting natural effect. Structures change from simple designs into supporters of environmental equilibrium, using feasible elements, for example, green rooftops, water gathering, and latent sunlight based plan.

The charm of mechanical headway, while driving advancement in different fields, frequently comes at the expense of natural corruption. Ecological supportability in innovation requires a takeoff from the direct "take-make-arrange" model towards a roundabout economy. The appeal of the most recent contraptions is presently blended with contemplations of item life span, repairability, and mindful removal.

Consider a tech organization focused on maintainability, where the charm of state of the art development coincides with drives to diminish electronic waste. Items are planned with secluded parts, making fixes and updates doable. The appeal of the most recent cell phone is upgraded by the information that its creation sticks to moral work rehearses, and its finish of-life removal is overseen capably.

In the transportation area, the charm of versatility is being reshaped by the standards of natural manageability. Electric vehicles gain conspicuousness as options in contrast to customary ignition motor vehicles, diminishing discharges and reliance on non-renewable energy sources. Practical metropolitan portability coordinates public transportation, cycling framework, and person on foot well disposed spaces, offering options in contrast to individual vehicle possession.

The idea of natural manageability penetrates the business scene, testing the charm of benefit augmentation to the detriment of environmental uprightness. Corporate manageability goes past charity to implant natural contemplations in business methodologies. The charm of a fruitful business is not generally estimated exclusively by monetary profits yet in addition by its commitments to social and ecological prosperity.

Consider a global enterprise focused on ecological supportability, where the charm of market predominance coincides with a commitment to diminishing its carbon impression. The organization puts resources into sustainable power, takes on roundabout economy rehearses, and participates in straightforward revealing of its ecological effect. The charm of its items is upgraded by the confirmation that mindful strategic policies support each part of the store network.

Ecological supportability broadens its impact into the style business, testing the charm of quick design — a model portrayed by fast creation cycles and dispensable dress. Manageable style stresses moral obtaining, fair work rehearses, and a shift toward roundabout design. The charm of trendy clothing is combined with a guarantee to diminishing material waste, advancing cognizant utilization, and cultivating a more fair industry.

In the domain of ranger service, ecological manageability turns from manipulative logging rehearses towards feasible backwoods the executives. The appeal of lumber and wood items is at this point not inseparable from deforestation however is laced with dependable collecting, reforestation endeavors, and the protection of biodiversity. Maintainable ranger service turns into a harmony between addressing human necessities and defending the trustworthiness of biological systems.

The charm of the travel industry, a significant worldwide industry, goes through a change inside the structure of natural maintainability. Manageable the travel industry stresses mindful travel, limiting the effect on normal and social assets. The charm of outlandish objections is not generally disengaged from contemplations of protection, local area commitment, and the conservation of novel environments.

Consider an eco-accommodating hotel settled in a biodiverse district, where the charm of a lavish escape coincides with a guarantee to natural stewardship. The retreat coordinates reasonable structure rehearses, upholds neighborhood preservation drives, and connects with visitors in instructive projects. The appeal of the excursion experience is advanced by the information that it contributes emphatically to the safeguarding of the general climate.

Marine protection turns into a point of convergence in the domain of ecological maintainability, testing the charm of overfishing and disastrous fishing rehearses. Supportable fisheries the board looks to adjust the charm of bountiful fish with the need to keep up with solid marine biological systems. Practices like dependable reaping, marine safeguarded regions, and hydroponics inside natural cutoff points become foremost.

With regards to energy creation, the charm of plentiful energy is re-evaluated inside the boundaries of ecological manageability.

Sustainable power sources, for example, sunlight based, wind, and hydropower, gain unmistakable quality as options in contrast to petroleum derivatives. The charm of energy freedom is combined with the obligation to relieve environmental change, decrease air contamination, and progress towards a low-carbon future.

The charm of water assets, when seen as boundless, is currently perceived inside the system of natural supportability. Supportable water the board goes past the charm of plentiful freshwater to consider the conservation of sea-going biological systems, evenhanded admittance to clean water, and the alleviation of water shortage. Preservation rehearses, wastewater reusing, and watershed insurance become vital parts of capable water use.

Natural manageability broadens its impact into instruction, testing the appeal of traditional learning models that might ignore environmental contemplations. Manageable instruction underlines an all encompassing comprehension of the interconnectedness between human social orders and the climate. The charm of information is interwoven with a consciousness of ecological difficulties, cultivating an age of people prepared to resolve squeezing worldwide issues.

Consider an earth centered educational plan where the appeal of scholarly accomplishment is supplemented by a comprehension of natural standards. Understudies take part in maintainability projects, partake in local area ecological drives, and graduate with a feeling of obligation towards the planet. The charm of schooling is improved by its job in forming naturally cognizant and socially capable residents.

The charm of biodiversity, frequently eclipsed by natural surroundings obliteration and environmental change, is a point of convergence of ecological supportability. Protection endeavors try to save the assortment of life on The planet, perceiving the natural worth of environments and the administrations they give. The charm of interesting species and biological systems is combined with a guarantee to living space safeguarding, rebuilding, and the relief of dangers to biodiversity.

The idea of natural supportability stretches out to squander the board, testing the charm of an expendable culture. Reasonable waste practices focus on decrease, reuse, and reusing. The charm of customer items is not generally disconnected from contemplations of their finish of-life influence.

9.4 Balancing Opulence with Purpose

In this present reality where the quest for extravagance frequently becomes the overwhelming focus, there is a developing acknowledgment that genuine satisfaction comes from offsetting extravagance with a feeling of direction. The charm of material riches and luxurious encounters, when the sole markers of progress, is being rethought for a more nuanced comprehension of living a significant and deliberate life.

At the core of this shift is the affirmation that richness, when separated from reason, can turn into an empty pursuit — an interminable mission for more without an unmistakable comprehension of why. The appeal of extravagance, whether as very good quality belongings or elite encounters, is being examined from the perspective of direction, provoking people to scrutinize the more profound significance and effect of their decisions.

Think about an effective business person who, in the wake of gathering critical riches, considers the charm of plushness in his life. He starts to address whether the quest for material achievement alone is sufficient to bring enduring fulfillment. In this contemplative excursion, he finds a longing for reason — a craving to contribute definitively to society, to have a beneficial outcome, and to leave a heritage past the gathering of riches.

In the domain of business, the idea of corporate social obligation (CSR) arises as a strong structure for offsetting plushness with reason. Organizations perceive that the charm of benefit committing to moral strategic policies, ecological manageability, and commitments to the prosperity of the networks they serve. Reason driven organizations focus on values over simple monetary profit, adjusting their missions to cultural and natural necessities.

Consider an extravagance style brand that, past the charm of high fashion, coordinates supportability into its plan of action. The brand sources materials morally, support fair work rehearses, and participates in magnanimous drives. The charm of style is not generally bound to the feel of the pieces of clothing yet is upgraded by the brand's obligation to having a beneficial outcome on both the business and the world overall.

With regards to self-improvement, people are progressively looking for a feeling of direction that heads past the collection of riches and status. The appeal of personal growth reaches out to developing significant connections, encouraging individual prosperity, and adding to the government assistance of others. Reason driven living turns into a core value, guiding people from the shallow features of progress toward a more valid and satisfying presence.

Think about a powerful leader who, notwithstanding making critical expert progress, ends up scrutinizing the charm of a determined quest for company pecking order climbing. Looking for reason, he investigates roads for rewarding the local area, coaching youthful experts, and advocating social causes. The charm of a reason driven life becomes extraordinary, bringing a feeling of satisfaction that rises above the accomplishments of his vocation.

In the domain of schooling, the charm of information is rethought inside the setting of direction driven learning. Instructive establishments focus on all encompassing turn of events, underlining scholastic greatness as well as the development of values, decisive reasoning abilities, and a feeling of social obligation. The charm of schooling is not generally bound to degrees and honors however stretches out to the long lasting excursion of individual and cultural development.

Think about a school that, notwithstanding scholarly educational plan, integrates programs zeroed in on local area administration, natural mindfulness, and moral initiative. The appeal of learning is advanced by encounters that expand points of view, ingrain compassion, and engage understudies to contribute definitively to the world. Reason driven schooling turns into an establishment for supporting mindful and empathetic worldwide residents.

The idea of offsetting richness with reason stretches out to the domain of altruism, testing the appeal of conventional beneficent giving. Reason driven magnanimity goes past composing checks to effectively captivating in friendly and natural causes. People and associations try to comprehend the underlying drivers of issues, team up with networks, and drive fundamental change. The charm of generosity isn't simply in that frame of mind of giving yet in the purposeful quest for positive, feasible effect.

Think a the about a donor, past the charm of conventional magnanimity, submerges herself in grasping the intricacies of social issues. She cooperates with associations, utilizing her assets and skill to address underlying drivers instead of only tending to side effects. The charm of direction driven magnanimity lies in its capability to impact groundbreaking change and add to the making of a more fair and just society.

In the domain of extravagance travel, the appeal of rich excursions is reclassified from the perspective of direction driven the travel industry. Explorers look for encounters that give unwinding and guilty pleasure as well as cultivate social trade, support neighborhood economies, and add to natural preservation. The charm of movement is presently not exclusively about idealism yet is interwoven with a feeling of obligation and a longing to leave a good effect on the objections visited.

Consider an extravagance resort that, as well as offering rich facilities, incorporates manageability rehearses, draws in with neighborhood networks, and supports protection drives. The charm of a get-away encounter is uplifted by the information that it lines up with standards of capable the travel industry, leaving insignificant ecological effect and contributing decidedly to the prosperity of neighborhood occupants.

The mix of direction in individual budget difficulties the appeal of materialistic utilization. Reason driven monetary arranging includes adjusting spending and venture decisions to one's qualities and long haul objectives. The charm of monetary achievement isn't exclusively estimated by the collection of riches yet is weaved with the deliberate utilization of assets to make a significant and intentional life.

Think about a person who, rather than surrendering to the appeal of obvious utilization, decides to put resources into encounters, schooling, and drives that line up with individual qualities. The charm of monetary prosperity is re-imagined as a device for making positive change, supporting significant undertakings, and adding to the improvement of society.

The idea of offsetting richness with reason reaches out to the domain of health and taking care of oneself. The charm of individual prosperity isn't bound to actual appearance yet envelops mental and close to home wellbeing, care, and a feeling of direction. People look for practices and ways of life that advance actual wellbeing as well as add to an all encompassing feeling of prosperity.

Consider a wellbeing retreat that, past the charm of spa medicines, consolidates care rehearses, nourishing schooling, and open doors for self-reflection. The charm of prosperity is interlaced with a guarantee to encouraging internal equilibrium, versatility, and a more profound association with one's motivation. Reason driven wellbeing turns into an extraordinary excursion that reaches out past actual wellbeing to incorporate the general personal satisfaction.

In the domain of innovation and development, the charm of state of the art progressions is offset with moral contemplations and a feeling of direction. Reason driven tech advancement focuses on arrangements that address cultural difficulties, advance inclusivity, and limit negative ecological and social effects. The charm of development isn't only in its oddity yet in its capability to add to everyone's benefit.

Consider a tech organization that, past the charm of the most recent devices, puts resources into projects resolving squeezing worldwide issues, like environmentally friendly power, computerized incorporation, and medical services openness. The charm of mechanical development is elevated by its arrangement with a more extensive reason — to use innovation for positive social change and manageable turn of events.

Natural manageability turns into an indispensable piece of offsetting extravagance with reason, testing the appeal of unreasonable utilization and ecological corruption. Reason driven living incorporates decisions that limit natural impressions, support economical practices, and add to the protection of the planet. The charm of a reason driven life is interlaced with a promise to ecological stewardship and the prosperity of the Earth.

Think a the about a person, past the charm of comfort, embraces a moderate way of life, lessens waste, and goes with practical decisions in everyday living. The appeal of direction driven supportability lies in the purposeful work to live as one with nature, perceiving the interconnectedness between private decisions and the wellbeing of the planet.

In the corporate world, the coordination of direction challenges the charm of benefit boost at any expense. Reason driven organizations focus on the prosperity of all partners, including representatives, clients, networks, and the climate. The charm of business achievement is reclassified as a power for positive change, adding to cultural prosperity and tending to worldwide difficulties.

Think about an organization that, past the charm of monetary achievement, effectively takes part in drives to advance variety and consideration, decrease its natural effect, and reward the networks it serves. The charm of direction driven business lies in its ability to be an impetus for positive social change, making an expanding influence that stretches out past the meeting room to impact the more extensive cultural scene.

www.ingramcontent.com/pod-product-compliance
Lightning Source LLC
LaVergne TN
LVHW021822060526
838201LV00058B/3480